STORIES FROM EVERYWHERE

An Anthology

STORIES FROM EVERYWHERE

This book is a collection of work written by students who participated in the October 2016 presentation of the Open University's Advanced Creative Writing course. All of the pieces that appear within remain the intellectual property of the author and are published as part of this anthology on a non-exclusive basis.

All of the authors have donated their work without charge and all proceeds from sales of this collection will be donated to charity.

ISBN: 978-1984340801

First Edition: February 2018

CONTENTS

INTRODUCTION

By Gareth Coates

This book is composed entirely of work written by students who participated in the October 2016 presentation of the Open University's Module A363: Advanced Creativing Writing

All of the authors whose writing appears on the following pages were in the equivalent of the third year of an Undergraduate Degree and combining their studies with all manner of other commitments and challenges. Some have been published elsewhere but for others, this anthology is their first published work.

These pieces – all written during the 2016-17 Academic Year – showcase the various genres covered by the course. You will therefore find fiction, poetry, script writing and life writing within this book.

With this in mind, determining how best to present the 20 contributions was something of a challenge; it seemed fairest to set them out in alphabetical order by author surname.

I would like to thank all of my fellow students who completed the course, whether they contributed to this anthology or not. I know that, for all of us, the course was as challenging as it was rewarding but the support that we showed each other whether through social media, OU forums, tutorials or other was tremendous and ultimately raised the standard of the writing you are about to read.

This book would not have been possible without the skill and dedication of Sara Donaldson, who in addition to making a contribution of her own has edited the texts that follow. Thank you Sara!

Finally, thank you for purchasing this book. In addition to showing support to talented writers, you have made a donation to charity. All of the contributors have donated their work without charge and ensured that any proceeds from the sale of this collection are donated to a good cause.

I sincerely hope you enjoy it!

THE GOLDEN CHALICE

A work of fiction, by Ashley Ablitt

Corinna stumbled over a lump hunched at the foot of the steps, landing heavily on the cold, cobbled stones. In the darkness, something metallic rolled close to her. She sat up, squinting through the dank and gloomy night. Behind, a weak light issued from the dark hulk of the monastery and she spotted a small boy curled up by the icy bottom step. She put out a tentative hand towards him and felt him shivering.

'Are you alright?'

'Yes, Miss,' murmured a faint voice.

Corinna breathed a sigh of relief and tried to stand. Pain shot through her foot and she cried out.

'Are you hurt?' He leaned towards Corinna, his dark curls framing a timid face. 'I'm really sorry, Miss. Let me help you to stand.'

'I think it's my ankle.' Corinna winced as she reached out towards the boy. Her hand curled around the sharp bone in his shoulder and she snatched her hand away in horror. He was so thin and so young, and looked hardly tall enough to reach her waist. What was he doing out here in the middle of nowhere? The monastery was the only habitation for miles around and that night the snow lay deep around the surrounding fields. The boy leant down and retrieved a cloth bag. Something metallic jingled inside.

'Don't worry, I'll be fine. What's your name?'

'James.'

Corinna frowned. 'What are you doing out so late at night? You should be at home with your family.'

'I'm looking for my mother. Can you help me?'

Corinna pursed her lips and looked about her. The wind had risen and in the pale light she saw snowflakes fluttering in the air. Was this weather ever going to break? She looked back at the boy. His stood rigid beside her, his fists tightly clenched and his bottom lip pushed out. He would never make it back to town if the snow continued. Her heart sank. She had slept little over the past couple of days, with the constant threat of the recent monastery closures that put hers and the monks' livelihood in jeopardy. Yet she could not leave James outside.

'Come on,' she urged, taking his hand 'let's go inside.'

Corinna opened a wide door and hobbled down a narrow dimly lit passage, trying not to lean on James. A candle at the far end provided just enough light to see the uneven stone floor.

'Where are we?'

'Sshhh, don't make a sound.'

Corinna led the way through an open doorway to a room on the right.

'What's that awful smell? I don't like it here.'

'It's a potion. Let's go quickly before the infirmarian returns.'

'Who?'

'I'm his assistant.'

Corinna pointed James towards a door on the opposite side of the room and picked up a lighted candle from a wooden bench.

'Through here,' she urged.

The passage was cold and dark but she drew him into a small

room on the left, pulling the door closed. A narrow bed and a cupboard were the only furniture. James rushed to stand in front of the fire burning in the grate.

'It's late but I may find some leftover food in the kitchen. Tomorrow we will look for your mother.'

Corinna returned shortly with a chunk of stale bread and a pitcher of water. James was fast asleep in front of the fire. She wondered where his mother was. Surely she would not leave her son to fend for himself? She covered him with a thin blanket from her bed and watched him awhile before falling asleep.

Corinna woke at dawn to find James had disappeared and so had the food. Her heart flipped in her chest. What if he was seen by any of the monks? She chewed on her thumb for a moment, then left the room and limped into the infirmary. Footsteps sounded outside the door and Brother Edward, the infirmarian, entered. His face was grave.

'Corinna, can you watch the potion for me,' he indicated the pot burbling over the fire, 'and check on Brother Thomas while I go to see the Abbot. There was a burglary last night. It appears that someone broke into the church and stole a golden chalice. Have you heard or seen anyone around the monastery?'

Corinna turned away as panic rose up inside her and she clutched her hands in a tight fist. This may be the end of the monastery, of her job.

'Corinna, did you hear what I said?'

'I'll do that, sir, but –.'

'Thank you.' Brother Edward raced from the room. Corinna let out a shaky breath. Calm down, she thought, I need to think clearly.

She gave the potion a stir then peeked into the room opposite, only to see Brother Thomas snoring heartily. She returned to the infirmary and then checked in her room. There was still no sign of James. Where had he gone? She remembered there had been a metallic sound when he had picked up his bag last night. Could he have taken the chalice? Surely not. But if so, why?

It seemed an eternity before Brother Edward returned. Corinna sat at the table in the infirmary gnawing at her fingernails, her heart fluttering widely and her hands clammy with sweat. He was still solemn, yet at once he noticed how pale Corinna was and chided her.

'Corinna, what is wrong? You look ill.'

James' small helpless face popped into her head. 'I am just a little tired, Sir, and my ankle is hurting a little. I slipped on the steps last night.'

'You must be careful. With all this snow, it will get very icy. Here, let me look at it.'

Corinna lifted up her leg and he felt around her ankle. She winced as he prodded the tender area.

'Looks like it's only a sprain, but I will bandage it for you and give you something to ease the pain, then I want you to lie down and rest.'

'But sir –'

He held up his hand. 'We are not too busy. I can take care of things around here.'

Corinna lay down on her bed for most of the day. Initially restless, the potion soothed her and she slept until nightfall.

The creaking of the door woke her, and in the light cast by the fire, she saw James come into the room. Behind him was a young woman. As James moved towards her she caught the glint of metal from the firelight. He was clutching the golden chalice. Suddenly Corinna was wide awake and sat up in bed.

'I've found my mother,' he said motioning to the woman following him. Corinna recognised her as one of the kitchen servants.

'Where did you go, James? I've been worrying about you all day.'

The boy hung his head.

The young woman stepped forward. 'I'm sorry to have troubled you, Miss. It's just that I've not had a chance to go home and visit James since the weather turned bad, so he came to see me instead. I'm afraid he took the chalice. He thought that if we kept it, I wouldn't have to work here anymore and could be at home with him.'

Corinna looked at the two of them and emotion tightened her throat. She blinked back tears.

'I'm afraid everyone is looking for the thief. You're not safe here.'

'I said to James that he shouldn't have taken it, so we've brought it here. Miss, please help us. We don't want to cause any trouble.'

Corinna looked thoughtful for a moment. 'We must return the chalice to the church immediately. It's dark and if everyone is at dinner, we can go now.'

Corinna swept back her cover and swung her feet to the ground.

James looked up, a note of determination on his thin face. 'I took the chalice and I will return it. I never meant any harm, Miss,

I'm sorry.'

Corinna smiled, relief surging through her.

The woman came closer. 'As the snow has eased off, James and I will be able to return home in the morning. Thank you for letting James stay here last night.'

'You're welcome.'

They turned without another word and left the room.

Corinna shivered and climbed back under her threadbare covers. Yet sleep evaded her.

She jumped at the sound of the door opening. Brother Edward came into the room with a tray.

'Corinna, how are you feeling? A little better, I hope.'

'Much better, Sir. Thank you.'

He nodded. 'Good. I have brought you food and wine as you have been asleep most of the day and I would like you to get plenty of rest.'

'But what about my duties?'

Brother Edward smiled. 'Don't worry, I can handle those for now. If necessary, one of the monks can help me, now that they don't have to continue their search for the chalice. Somehow, it has been returned to the church.'

Corinna felt her body sag with exhaustion. She reached for the tray, suddenly very hungry.

'Sleep well.' The door closed.

'Oh, I will' she replied, her grin spreading widely across her face.

MR. JAMES

A script, by Stephen Brown

FADE IN:

INT. CLASSROOM. DAY

The CHILDREN, all around 15 years old, shout and laugh. They congregate around desks in large groups.
MR. JAMES (early 50s) stands at the front of the classroom. His face is red. Sweat covers his brow.
Mr. James' wide eyes dart around the room, they beg for help or a symbol of hope from anywhere.

> MR. JAMES
> (barely audible)
> Please ... please, children. Be quiet.

Mr. James watches them as they ignore him.

> MR. JAMES
> For goodness sake ...

A GIRL looks over to Mr. James and laughs hysterically.
Mr. James mops his brow with a handkerchief.
A MATURE BOY, stubble, tall, muscular, stares at Mr. James with menace.
Mr. James stumbles forward. His hand clenches around the edge of a desk. He steadies himself then takes a deep breath.
The sound of children's chatter and laughter surrounds Mr. James. Engulfs him.
Mr. James' right hand trembles as he stands in front of the mature boy. A face off.
Silence ...

> MATURE BOY

What you lookin' at?

MR. JAMES
Get back to your desk.

The boy looks around him and laughs.

MATURE BOY
Are you going to fuckin' make me, like,
old man?

A chorus of gasps and laughter from all around.
Mr. James looks around the classroom. Panic in his eyes.

MR. JAMES
All of you. Get back to your desks.
Right now.

Mr. James claps his hands loudly in a last ditch effort to create some
sort of order. He walks in a small circle around the room.
A rolled up piece of paper hits Mr. James on the side of the head.
Mr. James lunges in the direction that the projectile came from. His
arms wide open in an effort to grab the child, or any child.
The children run away from him with ease. Some giggle. Some
scream.
Mr. James lunges in the opposite direction and bumps into the
mature boy.
The mature boy squares up to Mr. James.

MATURE BOY
Calm down, man. Just–

Mr. James pushes the mature boy with both hands.
The mature boy falls backwards on to the floor.
Mr. James stares down at the child. Closes his eyes.

INT. SCHOOL WAITING ROOM. DAY

Mr. James' blank eyes stare straight ahead.
Dressed in a crisp white shirt, tie and suit, he is the only person waiting in the room. The only other person present is the RECEPTIONIST, sat behind her desk.
The shiny shoe of Mr. James' right foot taps an abstract rhythm on the hard wood floor.
Mr. James looks to the door marked 'HEADMASTER', then to his wrist watch.
He looks directly at us and lets out a long, exhausted sigh. He breaks the fourth wall.

> MR. JAMES
> I suppose you're thinking I'm a
> monster.

He pauses for a moment, as if he is waiting for a reply. Finally ...

> MR. JAMES
> Or a maniac, perhaps? Someone
> should lock me up and throw away the
> key, no?

He reaches into the inside pocket of his suit jacket and pulls out a piece of paper. His eyes scan it.

> MR. JAMES
> An assault. That's what they're
> describing it as. Do you believe that?

He folds the paper back up with care and returns it to the inside pocket of his jacket.
Mr. James looks to either side then lowers his voice conspiratorially with a hint of a smile.

> MR. JAMES
> He had it coming to him if you ask me.
> I think you'd agree with me too if
> you'd been around here for the

amount of years I have. Seeing the
place slide into the swamp. Seeing
society slide into the swamp. You
should hear what the other teachers
say about the little bast–

Mr. James stops himself. A guilty expression appears upon his face.

> MR. JAMES
> No, a little discipline never did me any
> harm.

INT. BEDROOM. NIGHT

The shape of a small figure, covered in a duvet, lies on top of the
bed.
Just the red, teary eyes of a YOUNG MR. JAMES (12) can be seen as
they stare out of a crack in the duvet.
The door opens and MR. JAMES SNR (mid 40s) strides into the
room.
Mr. James Snr pulls the blanket from his son and yanks him from
the bed.

> MR. JAMES
> (V.O.)
> We had a little thing called respect.
> You would never catch me back-
> chatting, or swearing, or ...

On a desk in the room, a child's painting of a sunny day. Grass, blue
sky, the sun ...
The sound of a leather strap hitting with a thud.
A child's cry.

INT. SCHOOL WAITING ROOM. DAY

A bright sun in the blue sky is visible through a window. A perfect
summer's day.

Mr. James looks at the window. His gaze distant.

> MR. JAMES
> And they call this an assault?

He returns his attention to us. Focused. Certain.

> MR. JAMES
> If anything they should be
> congratulating me for giving the boy
> what he's needed for some time.

He keeps an intense stare on us for a long beat.
Finally, his gaze softens. Mr. James shakes his head and chuckles.

> YOUNG BOY
> (O.S.)
> Who are you laughing at?

Mr. James snaps his gaze to his right. A YOUNG BOY (12), in a
school uniform, sits in the seat beside him. The child looks angry
and defensive.

> YOUNG BOY
> Come on, who are you laughing at?
> Are you laughing at me?

Mr. James gives us a puzzled look then turns his attention back to
the boy.

> MR. JAMES
> Can I help you, young man? Shouldn't
> you be in class?

> YOUNG BOY
> Shouldn't you be in class?

> MR. JAMES
> Don't be cheeky, boy.

Mr. James stands and looks up and down the corridor. His stature one of supreme confidence and superiority.

MR. JAMES
Now, which class should you be in? I'll
take you there my–

Mr. James turns his gaze back to the boy but he is no longer there.
He squints his eyes in an act demonstrating his confusion then looks back up the corridor.
In the distance, the boy stands with his middle finger raised and his tongue poking out of his mouth.
Mr. James' face grows red and his brow lowers into a scowl. He marches towards the boy.
As Mr. James walks past the receptionist's desk she raises her head.

RECEPTIONIST
Mr. James, can I help you?

Mr. James marches on, his eyes only focused on the boy ahead of him.
The receptionist comes out from behind her desk and approaches Mr. James.

RECEPTIONIST
Whatever is the matter? You look
positively fuming.

MR. JAMES
The boy.

The receptionist follows Mr. James' gaze.

RECEPTIONIST
... boy?

MR. JAMES
The boy who is not in class. The boy
who is showing me no respect. The boy
... the boy ...

Mr. James stops walking and stares into the distance.
The hallway is empty. The boy is nowhere to be seen.
The receptionist puts a reassuring hand on Mr. James' shoulder.
Concern on her face.
Mr. James instantly pushes the hand away.

> MR. JAMES
> Nonsense. Nonsense, I tell you. A boy
> cannot simply dissapear –

> RECEPTIONIST
> Perhaps you would like to sit back
> down, Mr. James? I could get you a
> glass of water?

Mr. James raises his hand to his brow.

> HEADMASTER
> (O.S.)
> Mr. James ...

Mr. James turns sharply to face the HEADMASTER (mid fifties).
The headmaster stands in the threshold of his office. A solemn
expression on his face – dissapointment and concern for his senior
staff member.

> HEADMASTER
> If you don't mind ...

The headmaster gestures to his open door and then walks inside his
office.
Mr. James lowers his eyes to the ground.
He takes a deep breath then readjusts his tie and a determined
expression appears on his face.

INT. HEADMASTER'S OFFICE. DAY

The headmaster sits behind his desk. A large window behind him
shows the exterior of the school – a large playing field.

MR. JAMES
(O.S.)
Absolutely prepostorous. The boy is a
menace, a bully and a vacuum of every
teacher's patience and every student's
attention.

Mr. James sits on the edge of his seat. Upright and alert. An energy
in his eyes that makes him look considerably younger.

MR. JAMES
Sir, honestly, this boy – if you can call
a six foot two inch male, with a beard,
a boy – is the one that should be in
this office, not me. He grabbed my
arm. I merely pulled it away.

HEADMASTER
The boy's father has made a
complaint, Edward.

MR. JAMES
Well, he would, wouldn't he? That
doesn't make him right or me wrong.
The boy has most likely told his father
some cock and bull story in an effort to
gain his ...

Mr. James' attention moves from his conversation with the
headmaster and to the window.
The young boy from the waiting room stands outside the window
with a big cheesy grin on his face.
Mr. James' face darkens. His eyes rage.

HEADMASTER
(O.S.)
I do hear what you're saying, Edward,
I really do, but there has been a
complaint. Procedures must be

followed. Investigations made.

The young boy puts his nose against the window whilst staring in at Mr. James.
Mr. James' face in a grimace. The headmaster continues speaking but his words are merely a murmer in the background. Mr. James' breath, his heartbeat, are the predominant sounds.

EXT. GARDEN. DAY

The young Mr. James stands in the middle of the lawn and kicks a football against the wall of a brick outhouse. (Note: it is now revealed that the young Mr. James and the Young boy are the same person).
The rhythmic thud of the leather football hitting the brick wall is almost hypnotic.
The smile on young Mr. James' face as he controls the ball then kicks it back against the wall.
Suddenly, and breaking the trance like state, a door flies open and Mr. James Snr darts out.

> MR. JAMES SNR
> What the bloody hell do you think
> you're doing?

Mr. James Snr grabs his son forcefully by the arm causing him to cry out in pain.

> MR. JAMES SNR
> You need to learn a little thing called
> respect, my boy.

He throws him into the house then follows inside.
The football lies abandoned on the lawn.

INT. HEADMASTER'S OFFICE. DAY

Mr. James stares blankly out of the window.

> HEADMASTER
> Mr. James ... Mr. James, are you
> alright?

Mr. James blinks his eyes in quick succession and looks to the headmaster. Embarrasment and confusion show on his face.

> HEADMASTER
> Kind of slipped away on me there,
> Edward. Are you okay?

Mr. James takes his handkerchief from his pocket and wipes some sweat from his brow.

> MR. JAMES
> Yes ... yes, I'm fine. Just a little warm
> in here, that's all. A little warm.

The headmaster lifts a jug of water and pours the liquid into two glasses. He offers one to Mr. James who takes it.

> HEADMASTER
> Has this been happening often,
> Edward? These ... blackouts?

> MR. JAMES
> I don't know what you're talking
> about, Sir. It's just a little warm. I went
> a little dizzy, that's all.

The headmaster takes a sip of his water, deep thought show in a furrowed brow.

> HEADMASTER
> Edward ... I would be lying to you if I
> said I hadn't heard the talk around
> school –

                    MR. JAMES
          Talk? What talk?

                    HEADMASTER
          Well, I had passed it off as just gossip,
          but –

                    MR. JAMES
          But? But what? Sir, if you have
          something to say, I would appreciate it
          straight up.

                    HEADMASTER
          Your behaviour. People have been
          talking about your strange behaviour.
          Talking to yourself. Sitting alone,
          staring into the distance. Your
          colleagues are concerned.

Mr. James shows a hint of embarassment.

                    HEADMASTER
          Like I say, I had passed it off as just
          talk but after seeing it first-hand I
          can't ignore it.

                    MR. JAMES
          Sir, please, this is all a
          misunderstanding. It was the boy.

Mr. James points to the window where the boy still stands. The
headmaster turns in his chair with a puzzled expression.

                    MR. JAMES
          He was outside in the corridor too.
          That is what all the commotion earlier
          was about.

The headmaster stands and walks to the window. He stares outside
for some time – only the pane of glass separates him from the boy.

Finally, he turns around and faces Mr. James. The boy behind him is no longer there.

> HEADMASTER
> Edward. You've worked at the school
> for what … twenty years?

> MR. JAMES
> Twenty-two years, actually sir, but I
> don't know what –

The headmaster raises his hand in a gesture asking for silence.

> HEADMASTER
> That length of service is commendable.
> You're a good teacher, but, things can
> get on top of all of us from time to
> time.

> MR. JAMES
> Sir, you can see the boy out there.
> Surely anybody would be distracted by
> that.

> HEADMASTER
> There's no one out there, Edward.

Mr. James shakes his head then gets to his feet. He walks to the window and points at the boy through it.
From the headmaster's point of view there is no boy.
The headmaster walks to his door and opens it.

> HEADMASTER
> Susan, could you come in here for a
> moment please?

The headmaster turns back to Mr. James, still standing by the window, and watches him closely.
The receptionist walks into the office.

                    RECEPTIONIST
          Yes, Sir, how can I help?

                    HEADMASTER
          Earlier, in the waiting room, who was
          present?

                    RECEPTIONIST
          I'm not sure what you mean, Sir.

Mr. James walks over to her.

                    MR. JAMES
          The boy. You saw the boy that was
          there. The boy who is now outside that
          window.

Mr. James points behind him to the window.
The receptionist looks to the headmaster.

                    HEADMASTER
          It's okay, Susan, just be honest.

                    RECEPTIONIST
          I only saw you in the waiting room,
          Mr. James. I can't see anyone outside
          the window either.

Mr. James, still pointing behind him, stares in disbelief at the
receptionist.

                    RECEPTIONIST
          I'm sorry. I don't know what else to
          say.

                    HEADMASTER
          Thank you, Susan. That will be all.

The receptionist offers Mr. James a sympathetic smile and then
turns to walk out the door. Before she exits she stops and turns

back.

                    RECEPTIONIST
          You've been decent to me over the
          years, Mr. James. I hope you get better
          soon.

She walks out of the office.
Mr. James slumps into his chair. Deflated. His gaze still on the
window.
The headmaster walks back to his chair and sits down.

                    HEADMASTER
          Now, this incident in your class, I want
          you to forget about it. Nobody was
          seriously hurt and I will take care of
          the boy's father. Under the
          circumstances I'm sure he will be
          understanding.

Out of the window, the boy moves onto the playing field and plays
with a football.

                    HEADMASTER
          A leave of absence is in order I believe.
          Time to give yourself a rest. I'm a
          strong believer in 'R and R' and I'm
          sure in a few weeks, or months, you'll
          be in a position to start thinking about
          coming back.

Mr. James' blank expression, looking out of the window, shows that
he is not hearing the headmaster. He's in another place. Another
time.

EXT. PLAYING FIELD / GARDEN. DAY

The young boy kicks the football in front of him. He chases after it.
Young Mr. James kicks the ball against the wall.

The young boy stops running. Looks up, fear in his eyes. He backs up a little.
Mr. James stands with his foot on the ball. He looks down at the boy.
A smile slowly grows on his face.
Mr. James kicks the ball back to the boy.
The young boy hesitates before kicking the ball back.
The two of them laugh as they kick the ball back and forth between themselves in the school playing field.

INT. HEADMASTER'S OFFICE. DAY

Mr. James, still slumped in his chair, stares straight ahead towards the window.
The headmaster stands over him, worry in his eyes.
He darts to the door.
Mr. James' glazed eyes reflect the scene of him and the boy playing football in the field.

FADE OUT.

THREE BALLERINAS

A piece of life writing, by Gareth Coates

I am cold, there is a dull ache where my feet used to be and the grey February sky looks as if it might expel rain, sleet or worse at any moment. The wind howls around me as I trudge down the street past a sequence of anonymous terraced houses, their red brick shells the only hint of colour against the clouds, the worn paving slabs and the faded asphalt of the road. But I can't be distracted by the weather or the complaints of my body. I have a job to do. So it is that a few minutes later I find myself at the door of a large building, set back from the main road and speaking into an intercom: 'Good afternoon. My name is Gareth Coates and I'm looking into residential care for my grandmother. Would it be possible to come in and have a look around?'

This was not how I'd intended to spend a week's annual leave. Nor had I intended to phone my employers and negotiate an extra three days of unpaid leave of absence.

As I arrived at Nana's house, darkness had fallen and it seemed like the house was deserted. There were no lights on anywhere and phone calls went unanswered. I tried both the front and back doors – locked – and searched fruitlessly for a spare key hidden somewhere. Then I reached for my phone and made another call.

'Dad, I can't get into Nana's house.'

'What are you on about?'

'She's not answering the door. There's no lights on. I can't find a key anywhere and she's not answering the phone.'

There was a silence between us that felt like it lasted for hours, although in reality it can only have been a second or two. Then Dad took charge, telling me in a voice heavy with concern that I had better call the police.

Within half an hour, a policeman had forced the back door open and we entered through the kitchen. The smell was the first thing that hit me; fetid, redolent of stale urine. The room looked as if it hadn't been entered in a couple of days. It didn't take long to find Nana, tucked up in bed, her white hair dishevelled, her hearing aid and glasses on the bedside table. Startled at the intrusion, she sat bolt upright to reveal that she was wearing her old beige overcoat and had forgotten not just that she had visitors but how to operate the central heating.

I contacted Social Services and various family members the following morning. A meeting involving a social worker took place that lunchtime where it was agreed that Nana would go into hospital for tests and observation and then go into residential care once the right location had been found.

I immediately volunteered to do the research into where Nana might go, reasoning that if we were to subject her to the one thing she was adamant she didn't want then the least we could do was get her into the best place.

The plan was simple enough; I would visit all the local care homes during the day and set the house straight during the evenings. I walked from place to place, arrived without warning and asked to look around. I tried to time my visits around mealtimes where possible, then made notes about what I had seen after I left.

As I trudged through Stockton-on-Tees, I thought about how Nana had fostered my love of football by taking me to Wembley

Stadium or by having a kickabout with me in the park. I determined to use the administrative skills learned through 15 years in the game to secure the best outcome for her. Always serious, bookish and good at building routines, I took a sort of grim pleasure in my task.

I drew up a schedule; grouping the various locations together to make the journeys manageable and setting myself the task of visiting three or four a day. Working to restore Nana's once pristine but now stained and stinking home to some sort of liveable state, I found a number of unpaid bills. I also found that Nana had been drawing her pension, and then secreting it about the house. There was a lot of cash in the house; I worked through the bills and started each morning in the Yorkshire Bank with envelopes stuffed with cash and paying in slips concealed inside my coat. Once I had cleared the queue at the bank, I would walk out of town, to start the day's visits.

That first home I visited – the one set back from the road – looked impressive from the outside, but once I entered I noticed that the entire building smelled of cabbage. It also looked like it had last been decorated at some time during the 1970s.

Another was clearly brand new; every surface was a brilliant white and the building's perfume was of a powerful disinfectant, with a hint of something unpleasant behind it. But there was nothing in any of the rooms to help residents to feel at home; no nick-knacks or personal effects. When I saw a nurse square-bashing a room full of residents, I knew that I would never allow Nana to live there.

None of the places I visited turned me away and I was always given a tour. On these tours, I listened to the woman guiding me around (it was always a woman) talk about the place and I would scan each room, making mental notes. I remember one converted house with terrifyingly-steep staircases and no locks on the doors and convincing myself that Nana would either break her neck or simply wander off, never to be seen again. I rejected another place because I saw staff serving lunch whilst clearing away the breakfast served hours earlier.

After each tour was concluded, I would retreat to a pub or café and write down my thoughts; these frantic bullet points formed the basis of a report I wrote for my family that helped us determine where Nana should see out her final days. An early experience in a café, where the smell of stale fat even permeated the grey dishwater that was apparently 'coffee' meant that, wherever possible, I found myself a pub in which to hide, particularly towards the end of each day when a pint of Strongarm or McEwan's 80 bob could help to restore flagging spirits.

Occasionally, as I scribbled into my notebook – bought specifically for the purpose – the conversations around me would stir me from my thoughts:

'Alright, gadge. See the game Sat'day?'

'Aye. Shite again. That daft apath Viduka's fuckin' useless man. Shouldn't've bothered, like. Six o'clock in the morning I was on that coach!'

'Chelsea are a good side, like.'

'Howay, man! We canna be gettin' beat 3-0 if we wanna stay up!'

As soon as I saw it, Victoria House was the only place I wanted Nana to be; it had specialist facilities for dementia sufferers and it was close to her house.

It had pictures of the town on the walls and it didn't smell of anything. Not bleach, not cabbage. It was just clean. Friendly, too. I saw a nurse take a resident by the arm, guide him into an activity room and bring him a cup of tea with a cheerful, 'how's that, pet?'

And so, Nana moved into her own room surrounded by some of the things she held most dear, including a bottle of Bols Gold Liqueur that contained a wind-up ballerina which danced to *The Blue Danube* as gold leaf cascaded down. Dad had brought it home from working in Germany. It was basically the world's poshest snow globe, but it was precious to us.

Over the next year, I travelled back to Stockton as often as I could to see Nana, but it was hard. My cousin, Jamie, was restoring Nana's house so that it could be rented out to pay for her care, so I had to stay elsewhere.

Worse still, Nana seemed to shrink and age before me every time I went and every trip was difficult. On one occasion, I caught a vomiting bug that had been doing the rounds of Victoria House. On the next, she didn't seem to recognise me at all for the first two days.

The last time I visited her, the 'old' Nana sprang back to life, just for a day. On my final trip to Victoria House we spent hours talking and reminiscing and she shared with me lots of memories; things we'd never talked about, like when Grandad used to take her dancing as a young woman and how much she'd loved it.

As I prepared to leave, she said to me: 'Would you please take me back to my house? I'd like to go home now.'

My heart sank. There was a long pause as I scrambled for what to say. I eventually decided that the only thing to tell her was the truth.

'Nana, I'm sorry, but this is where you live now. You were

struggling to manage on your own, so we got you some help. I know it's not what you want but it is very nice here.'

'I see. I understand. You did what you thought was best.'

A few days later, on 19th February 2007, I got a phone call from one of her nurses. 'Your nana's not well. She's been refusing to eat and drink but the doctor wants to take her to hospital. We thought we'd best ring you.'

'How long has she been refusing to eat or drink?'

'Since the day after you went home.'

In that moment, I was both heartbroken and relieved. Heartbroken because my grandmother – my lovely, caring, adventurous Nana – was reaching the end of her life and relieved because she had fought her way through the fog of dementia one last time to make a decision that I had a duty to honour. I asked to speak with the doctor, who insisted that due to dehydration, he had a duty to summon an ambulance for Nana and place her on a drip.

'Doctor, are you seriously telling me that an 89-year-old woman who has taken a decision not to eat or drink would benefit from being kept alive, against her will, alone in a hospital?'

'I have a duty to her as a patient to ...'

'Your job is to "do no harm". I am telling you that if you take her to hospital and keep her alive against her wishes, I'll report you for misconduct. The next time we speak will be at the GMC! I am asking you to respect Nana's decision and let her go.'

'Very well, Mr Coates. I understand.'

Lillian Louisa Coates passed away peacefully overnight, without going to hospital. For the funeral, I took the first flight from Heathrow that morning, then the last flight back in the evening. Dad had been adamant that the one thing of Nana's he wanted as a keepsake was the Bols Ballerina.

Despite the fact that I worked at Heathrow Airport at the time, it hadn't occurred to me that this family heirloom would fall foul of the regulations that prohibit airline passengers from carrying more than 100ml of liquid onto an aeroplane as hand luggage. I didn't have a bag and flatly refused to allow the bottle to be checked in to the hold to be smashed to pieces. Bamboozled, the person checking in the flight suggested I go to customs and speak with them.

The person operating the x-ray machine said that I couldn't take the bottle on to the plane to which I retorted that I wasn't getting on the plane without it.

'Sir, you can't take more than 100ml of liquid on the flight.'

I flashed the pass that, were I back in London, would have allowed me to walk straight onto the plane, without passing through customs.

'I know that. I work airside at Heathrow. But this isn't a bottle of spirits. It's a family heirloom.'

'But it does have liquid in it?'

'It also has a wind-up ballerina and pieces of gold leaf in it! Look, I'm not going to crack this thing open in mid-air and drink it. I'm flying home from my grandmother's funeral! My Dad brought this ballerina back from Germany 40 years ago and it is the only thing I'm taking back for him. I know the bloody rules. This thing is an antique!'

Eventually, the ballerina was wrapped in clear duty-free bags, carried on to the flight by the Captain and then presented to me with an instruction that it was to stay on my lap for the duration of the journey. I believe I am still the only person to bring more than 100ml of liquid onto a Heathrow-bound flight since that rule was brought in!

Nana would have liked that; she had always been slightly cussed, very determined and prepared to fight for her family. Dad treasured the Bols Ballerina until he died; it is now with my sister.

It's been a decade since Nana passed away but I still think about her a great deal. I remember the hours of walking through Stockton and how proud I was that the skills I had learned and taught myself – the routines, the note-taking, the obsessive project management – had helped me to support a woman I loved dearly and whose encouragement had spurred me on through difficult times. I think of the brilliant birthday I spent with Nana when I was about ten, first taking a tour of Wembley Stadium, then wandering around London Zoo. Curiously, I would spend a second birthday at London Zoo, more than two decades later, and I would again be in the company of Lillian Coates.

In July 2009, I became a father to a beautiful baby girl, who had always been destined to be named Lillian. At the moment she was born, the sun came out. In some ways, it has never gone back in.

Our Lillian is an active, curious and charming young lady who loves nothing better than to pirouette around the living room. She also loves to visit new places and to learn and I've lost count of the number of new places we have been to together.

The loss of a loved one is heart-wrenching; perhaps doubly so when that loss is preceded by an illness like dementia, which erodes the person's essence until almost nothing is left. Yet we find ourselves, in time, transcending the grief to retain happy memories and we honour those who have left us by bestowing their names on those who follow.

I don't think there's anything mawkish about this and I encourage my daughter to be her own person. Yet, occasionally, as she plans an adventure or dances around the room, I see a twinkle in her eye that is hers, yet somehow familiar.

THE SLEEP GIVER

A work of fiction, by Sara-Jayne Donaldson

Do you ever wonder why you do things? Why you go right instead of left, choose a bagel over a bun, say yes instead of no. Play God instead of leaving well enough alone?

I was heading to a new life. A new life with better prospects, the chance to make a life, save a life perhaps. Who knew? All I knew was that I had to get away and start afresh. Make something of myself and get away from the fog and fear of the city.

It was raining when I arrived, the tears of angels weeping down on me, clearing the dust from the lanes and washing away the sins of the late summer. I'd come from London, with its soot and grime and the beggars that grabbed you by the trouser cuffs and demanded to be heard. They'd look you in the eye and cry for help, for food, for money. 'Just a little, Mister, help a man on hard times'. But it was always hard times back there. I remember, once, I gave a man my last pound. A crisp pound note, all I had left to see me through the week. His skin was crusted with dirt, matted hair fell over his tired eyes, froth nestled into the corner of his mouth, evading the handkerchief he kept in his breast pocket for show. Those rheumy eyes spoke to me, reminded me what I might have been. He got my last pound.

When I saw him again, a few days later, sitting by the hospital door, he was clutching a brown paper bag. Those eyes still swimming, looking up to the passersby and selling the same line

STORIES FROM EVERYWHERE – AN ANTHOLOGY

'Just a little Mister.' Just a little? I'd given him a pound, enough to clean himself up and sort himself out for a while. I went hungry while he ... well, never mind. On my way home I gave him a sip from my bottle. I heard they found him by the canal.

'Mr Bell?'

'Sorry?'

A hand jabbed towards me, stiff and formal, as though she'd never seen the like of me before. The attempt at a handshake was endearing. The delicate hand, the pink nail polish hiding yellowed, stained nails that bled through, the absence of a wedding ring. Didn't she know you shook hands with your right? A leftie with no thought to the majority. I dropped my bag and grasped her hand in mine, a little too hard perhaps. She winced.

'Mr Bell? My name's Patricia, I'm here to take you to the Manor.'

A whistle, shrill and high-pitched parted the crowds. The station master turned slowly away as the train began to depart, chugging its way down the rusted trackway. The crowds dissolved. I felt the rain seeping into my neck, iced fingers blue against my collar.

Patricia was a sweet young thing once you got to know her. She'd been a nurse in that large hospital in Scotland, the one that disinfected the lads that came home from the war. The lads that shook and slurred as life blurred around them. They used kindness, and compassion and electricity. She said she'd never done that, but I know she had. Once when sitting, savouring a cigarette, we heard a scream, and a shudder ran through her. She covered her ears and curled forward, head to her knees. I held her then, just for a moment, but she didn't move. The ash curled from her cigarette, grey, dying as it fell to the ground and was swept away on the breeze. She just looked at me in the end, no words, just a haunting behind her eyes.

Life at the Manor was good. An upper-class establishment for the elderly and infirm, not your beggars or your idiots – they were still kept behind closed doors in white-washed buildings that smelled of carbolic soap, vomit and urine. No, this place was perfect. There were no operations to attend, no scrubbing of knives and probes, no holding down a patient until he passed out from the pain. No saws or hatchets or needles the length of your arm. Just a 'Good Morning, Mrs Elvington' as you poured the tea and smiled politely at the old dear. I'd fallen on my feet and intended to stay there.

I say no needles, but that's not entirely true. The Manor was fully stocked. A privately funded establishment must be fully equipped to deal with life's uncertainties. Even those on the cusp of death should be afforded the opportunity to stretch out their days. But then I found myself in the midst of 'the choke'.

I had barely been there for a month when a patient died. It was not unexpected, but it was particularly gruesome. I had not seen the like of it since I packed my bags and decided to leave the city. Old Man Williams had enjoyed his post-dinner cigar, like the true old-time gentleman that he was, and was entertaining the ladies with his tales of colonial bliss in the heat of the Indies.

'My dears, the living was decent, but the heat was unbearable at times.' He puffed on his cigar. 'The little lady just could not understand the pressures of a modern gentleman and his lifestyle,' putt, 'but I say, we had some parties ... '

As I turned towards the commotion Williams leant back in his seat, his hands, withered and dry, clawing desperately at his throat. His cigar gently smouldered through his trouser leg as it fell from his hands. Nurses rushed forward to wheel the others away. Desperate ladies upset at what was happening. Ladies desperate to see what was happening. Time stood still for me; there was a remembrance of what had gone before, of my old life. He was turning blue. Just a slight tinge as he gasped for breath, nails scraping through the course beard. His legs were sprawled, a kicking of the heel showing the stress as his breath fought to be released. Blood bubbled up, staining his spittle as it frothed. His hue changed as the poison in his body coursed through. A deep, dark, inky blue. I took the bottle from my pocket, soaked my handkerchief quickly, lest others should see, and held it to his nose. I cradled his head, pulling him to me. Like a child waking from a nightmare he pushed into my chest as I held him still. With one final kick and a gasping heave, he left.

As the months rolled on, Mr Williams was forgotten and the old ladies found another man to idolise. I kept myself to myself and did my work well. I was there to care for the elderly, so that's what I did. Few people asked me where I came from, fewer still asked me anything personal. It amazed me how someone could fit in so comfortably and so easily. Complete monsters were roaming the world, and their colleagues were likely oblivious to the evil in their midst. I kept myself thankful for the small things in life and prayed daily for the old people in our care. At least here they could live out their days in comfort, and I would be there to help them. My father never had that luxury, so I would honour his memory and be a dutiful son to those I served.

The old people got older, and with that came the frailties of old age. All around me I could see flesh wither and memories fade. I adored those I worked for: Mrs Witworth with her love of elderflower wine, Mr Elvington and his daily games of backgammon with Mr and Mrs Levy, Mrs Heselton who used to wander around the grounds, picking weeds and talking to her pet retriever that had died twenty years before. I was fascinated. As I cared for them I could see the gratitude in their eyes. They knew they had a friend, one who would listen to stories of their youth while dispensing pills and potions. Many never saw their family from one month to the next and it saddened me that these fine specimens of humanity were abandoned to relative strangers.

When winter arrived the Manor changed. My room was ice-cold as draughts seeped in around the window frames. The frosted patterns that spread out along the panes crept inside and covered the walls like a deadly, delicate lace. The cold froze my extremities. My fingers became numb, useless lumps, turning white in the night as the blood refused to circulate. The searing pain was almost unbearable as the deadening numbness gave way to boiling heat when the blood returned. My lips became bloody and raw as I bit down hard to smother the screams that threatened to escape them. It was then that I turned once again to the bottle, with its cloying, sweet smell. The sleep giver. A tiny drop would suffice when the pain became too much.

It was a Tuesday in mid-November when Gauri Phule, an Indian lady of many years residence, noticed blood on my lips and the tell-tale white ring finger on my left hand. She asked me how long I had had the Raynaud's affliction, taking my hands in hers and rubbing vigorously. Crooning an ancient lullaby she soothed my soul with her kindness. Her eyes twinkled in the light of the snow-filled morning.

'You are a kind man', she whispered to me.

She pulled me close, enveloping me in her soft, silken sari.

'Do not let me suffer.'

As I pulled back she held my gaze. She had given me her greatest gift. Permission.

She was my sweetest, my most perfect dispatch. There was no fuss or fear.

Her room was lavish. Deep hued silks and velvets anointed the dark wood and extravagant soft furnishings, dripping off the furniture like a shimmering liquid. A grandmother clock tickled the air with its gentle chimes as Guari reclined on her soft, feather bed. She held out her hand to take the glass I offered. I had decided on Port, a viscous, luscious liquid that was heavy enough to mask the stinging, sweet taste of the chloroform.

'It tastes bitter tonight, Bell, what have you given me?'

'Just a new variety, grandmother Gauri. Drink it down.'

'It certainly burns the throat more than usual.'

I took her glass and wiped it clean before placing it back on her nightstand. Then I watched as slowly, slowly her breath softened. She looked at me, one final time, a realisation softly rippled over her face, and she was finally at peace.

Patricia found me the next morning to tell of how the old lady had died in her sleep. We sat on the terrace, cigarette ash floating away towards the lake, as we recalled how she had loved life.

'You know, I don't understand how she died,' she said, 'she wasn't so old, or ill.'

I said nothing, just watched the breeze gently bend the weeping willow in the distance.

'She was in perfect health.'

I adjusted my jacket, taking a drag on my Navy Cut. The bottle nestled inside my pocket. The cold was nipping my hands and nose, while the familiar feeling of blood leaving my fingers was biting hard. My veins were made of ice.

'Does it matter how it happened? She's at peace now, let her go,' I flicked the remaining ash to the floor and ground the stub into the dirt. 'Come on, there are others who need our help in there.'

She didn't suspect a thing. Poor Patricia.

Five more residents died in their sleep. The director put it down to the unusually cold winter we'd been having. That was the beautiful thing about the sleep giver, it left no trace. No doctor or coroner could find a hint of the sweet death bringer. But it was bitter, Guari had reminded me of that. No, the best way was sometimes the simplest. Each poor unfortunate, whose eyes had begged me to help them, were relieved while they slept. A small nub of cotton wool, soaked in chloroform, was placed in each nostril, and within a short time, as I held their hands, the sweet spectre of death took them to Paradise. Once the wool was removed I threw it in the fire and left the room. The fire would burn away and in the morning the scene would be peaceful and calm for the maid.

No one knew what I had done. We all knew that the residents would eventually leave us. Leave us with beautiful memories of lives well lived. They now left us before decrepitude hit.

Do you ever wonder why you do things? Do you ever wonder how one, simple decision can change your life forever?

Early that morning I left my frozen room and settled in my usual place on the terrace. Filling my lungs with nicotine-laced smoke, life was good. I was doing good work. The hospital was far behind me and no one knew where I was. No one knew my name and Dr Bell, the myth, was now a valued member of the Manor's household. It was all as it should be.

'Penny for your thoughts?' Patricia stood before me, pretty as a picture. Her breath sparkled in the cold, frost-laden air.

'Love. Sex. Redemption.'

'Pardon?' she took a step backwards, laughing. And as she did so she started to stumble, I lurched forward to try to catch her, and a small blue bottle fell out of my jacket pocket. She froze. She had seen its like before, at the hospital, with her soldiers.

'Arthur, what's that?'

Why ask, she knew what it was. Her eyes widened as she took a step backwards. I picked up the bottle. She knew.

Instinct betrayed me. I grabbed her wrist, pulled her close and covered her lips with mine. A kiss as I pinned her arms behind her. I could give her one final gift. She went rigid, I pushed her against the wall, hard. With one hand, I took the bottle and soaked my handkerchief with sweet salvation. I gently bit her lip before slipping the soft, clean cotton over her mouth.

On a crisp January morning, I laid her by the weeping willow.

I had to leave, of course I did, though it pained me with all my heart. Patricia was found by Mrs Heselton and of course I had to sign the death certificate. Death by misadventure, hyperthermia had visited that morning, so it seemed. They said I left of a broken heart.

So, here I am. A new face in a new world. They say New York is enlightened. I turned right this morning as I entered the hospital grounds. Bellevue has a new doctor. Just call me Smith.

A SONNET AND SESTINA

Poetry, by Lorcan Duggan

The Cyclist – a Sonnet

The cyclist pedalled fast along the street
the traffic crawled much slower alongside,
I watched him pull away despite my beat
if I caught him, I could maybe save my pride
This cyclist he was cycling with one hand
a cell-phone in the other I supposed,
quite risky with such traffic all around
to take a call, just see the risk he posed!
Just then he dares an even bolder move,
left arm outstretched, he swings across the lane
between the cars, he steers as if to prove
no hands required! This cyclist is insane!
But then I see the nature of his plan,
my cyclist is in fact a one-armed man.

Driving to a Funeral – a Sestina

Our black Vauxhall Victor is a bastion on wheels.
The deep hum of engine vibration, a comforting sound
rising and falling, through confident gear changes.
The red polished bench seats, are for me a slide,
down Irish country roads, round corners
along hedgeways, going to a funeral, with my father driving.

I lie on the rear seat, and peer out the window, my father, driving

43

to his mother's funeral. The drawn-back windscreen corners
like a grimace, like my father's serious face. His strong hands slide
left, then right, confidently, on the red leather steering wheel's
surface, emitting a leathery scent, a squeaking sound,
as my view through the windscreen constantly changes.

My father's driving is always slow and boring, it never changes,
but this day is different. I watch the speedometer-needle slide
across the horizontal gauge, quivering as if nervous, at the speed we
are driving.
I have never seen my father drive so fast before. A crushed-gravel
sound
encroaches from outside. 'It's coming from the wheels',
my father explains, as he swings the Vauxhall Victor round the
corners.

My father turns his head to me and remarks tersely 'She corners
well'. As if to excuse his, out of character, roller-coaster driving.
I lie on the rear seat, and ponder the changes
my grandmother's death will bring. Have I heard for the last time
the soft sound
of her voice, encouraging me to cycle with my stabilisor wheels?
Encouraging me to venture up the high playground slide?

My eyes are big as I observe my four uncles slide
my grandmother's coffin into the earth. Tears sneak from the
corners
of my father's eyes. I squeeze his hand with mine. His expression
changes

to a struggling-smile. Afterwards, my uncle asks my father 'will you be driving
back today?' My father replies quietly 'yes, the wheels
of life must keep turning'. I wonder at how normal the brothers sound.

Returning in the car at night, with darkness and the soothing sound
of gentle country music, whispering from the radio. I feel my father's driving
is calmer, no need for hurry now. I slide
across, lie down, and watch the night sky as it changes,
the clouds race across the moon, the corners
of the windscreen frame my world in our bastion on wheels.

Our black Vauxhall Victor has its own sound, it is our bastion on wheels.
Its comforting hum suffers no changes, its bench seat a slide
in disguise. 'She corners well' I say to my father, when he takes me out driving.

SURFING THE SMUG

A piece of life writing, by Janet Floyer

Have you ever had to travel long-haul with young children – on your own? By the time they reach their teens and have opioid-based smart phones your life will be much easier, but before then it is hard labour. There will be moments of calm that feel like great achievements, but this is when you need to be on your guard. There is a sense of pride that sneaks up on you like a wave and turns into smugness. That is when things begin to go wrong. You have to learn to surf the wave, catch it and make it last. Ride the big kahuna of hubris for as long as possible. Like me, you might fail a few times. You'll wipe out as the wave crashes over you and you'll tumble, gasping for air as you struggle to the surface with your pants full of sand.

My family calls it Surfing the Smug.

I had my first Surfing lesson on a flight from London to Toronto with two toddlers in 1999. We lived in London, and flew back every summer to spend time with my family in Canada. I had done the journey before with my husband and one child, but this was to be my maiden voyage solo with two children. It would be a test of my mothering skills. Each time I thought about it my stomach clenched and my tongue went dry like a long, cracked riverbed in a drought.

My own mother had travelled a lot when I was young but when I asked her for advice she confessed that she never brought me with her. Once, I had screamed non-stop on a flight from New York to

Orlando and she never got over it. After that, my grandparents would come to stay so she could enjoy child-free trips to Europe with my father. I considered this idea, but frankly I think she would have been disappointed if I had arrived in Toronto without her grandchildren.

So I asked Barbara, my mother-in-law, who made several solo journeys with her children. Like me, she lived in London while her family was in Montreal. But her journeys were in the 1950s and she had to travel by ship. While I would have to endure an eight-hour flight, her journey took eight days. I was fairly certain she would give me no sympathy, but I thought she might have some useful advice.

I think Barbara started Surfing the Smug in her early 30s and has never once wiped out – or at least she never admitted it. Sitting in my kitchen one afternoon amidst the chaos of afternoon tea with the children I decided to ask for help.

'Barbara,' I said. 'How did you manage travelling by ship, alone with your children?'

'Well, I only ever travelled with one at a time. I had a seven year age gap, not twenty months. So many people on board had children. We always gave the children supper early at the first dinner seating, and then put them to bed. Then the adults would meet for cocktails and have dinner together at the second seating. It was really very social.'

'Hmmm ... so maybe I should leave one of them with you?' I said passing her the youngest as I gave the table a wipe.

'Try to talk to people, it passes the time,' she said ignoring me. 'Mark was always so good, and the secret I think was I always travelled with his mattress because I thought it would make him feel at home.'

I imagined Barbara arriving in Montreal onboard the elegant Carinthia with steamer trunks, a toddler, and a rectangular mattress hitched up on her back like some kind of latter day ninja turtle.

'Maybe there will be an outbreak of chickenpox at nursery school and I can cancel the flight,' I said collecting our mugs.

Departure day finally arrived, and my husband waved us off at Heathrow. I was alone with two little girls, a double-buggy, and a lot of clobber. In the end I had decided against bringing their mattresses – there just wasn't room. I did, however, bring along some carrot sticks, a story book, and a new toy each. We boarded early and I was grateful to British Airways to be in the bulk-head seats. A woman about my age with a baby sat opposite. A kindred spirit! We could put the children to bed early and drink cocktails together for the rest of the journey! She was alone too, but I could tell she was too preoccupied to chat just yet because her baby was a little restless.

I remember this part of the journey fondly; the clouds gave way to blue skies and sunshine streamed in through the little oval windows as we climbed higher and left grey and drizzly London behind us. My daughters were quiet, like two peaceful little Buddhas paying attention as I read them a new story. I felt myself begin to relax and I thought I had been a little silly dreading the flight; I could do this!

I think it was around the time the stewardess handed out the Sky-Flyers Activity Packs that my neighbour's baby started to howl, while mine focused quietly on a new game. I felt a warm wave of self-satisfaction begin to envelop me like a mother's hug and I sat proudly between my two children, and caught the eye of the other mother. I gave her a sympathetic smile, and felt a flash of schadenfreude as her baby began to howl and stood up to rock him while the stewardess installed the SkyCot.

As I rode my wave of self-satisfaction my children became bored with the Activity Pack and I pulled out the emergency carrot sticks. They tired of these too, threw them to the floor and needed trips to the loo. It's not easy fitting three people into one of those little cubicles and I remember wondering how anyone managed to join the mile high club in one of them.

Walking back down the aisle I noticed a shift in the universe; the howling baby was quiet and the noise was now coming from my own two restless, over-tired children. I felt the wave begin to crest as the equilibrium continued to shift. The other mother's baby was sleeping soundly in its little cot. She gave a little shrug and smiled at me as she sipped the glass of champagne a stewardess had given her. I think it was a look of pity, with a dash of superiority.

While her baby slept for the duration of the flight, I spent the remaining seven hours in a frenzy of reading stories, colouring in, trips to the loo, and trying to make carrot sticks exciting. When we finally landed I looked and felt like I had been mauled by the Wave of Smug; my clothes were rumpled, my hair was a mess, and I was surrounded by children's detritus.

As the aeroplane arrived at our gate, I finally got the courage to talk to the other mother.

'You are so lucky!' I said leaning across the aisle. 'How did you do that?'

'I gave him Phenergan,' she whispered with a smile. 'My mother recommended it.'

It was a year before I would have to do that journey again, and I spent a lot of time dreading it. Barbara came for tea again, and told me about other gruelling but fun journeys she had made. On one train trip from London to the south of France, she ended up sharing her couchette with another woman who had noisy, restless children with her.

'What did you do?' I asked.

'I gave all the children sleeping tablets – I told them they were sweeties,' she said.

'You drugged them!?' I asked in a mix of awe and horror. 'Weren't you afraid something might happen to them? What if it had the reverse effect? What if they couldn't wake up?'

'Oh, I only gave them a half. It was a lovely trip. The other lady and I had dinner together, she was very interesting. And you know, we slept very well,' she said, sipping her tea with a smile as she remembered.

The following summer, I felt more prepared. I brought packs of Walker's Crisps, and mini Mars Bars wrapped like presents. This time I had a back-up plan, and I felt confident when my husband dropped us off at Heathrow.

The children were happy and we had the bulk-head seats again. When I felt the wave of smugness begin to swell underneath me I was ready for it. They played quietly with their Sky Activity Packs and I reached into my bag and pulled out a bottle of Phenergan and the measuring spoon our doctor had given me. With reckless abandon I measured out two teaspoons of pink syrup for my oldest, and one teaspoon for the little one.

I read them their favourite story until they fell into a wonderful, peaceful sleep. When the stewardess came over and handed me a glass of champagne saying 'well done you' I felt a sense of pride and took it gratefully. Opening up one of the magazines I brought for myself, I put my seat back and sipped it slowly, and Surfed the Smug uninterrupted for seven hours straight.

Of course, all good things come to an end and we eventually landed in Toronto. I organised our belongings and felt refreshed, but I had two small problems. Both children were so deeply asleep I couldn't wake them up.

The Stewardess who had given me the champagne, asked if she could help and I explained that the children were obviously exhausted by the Activity Pack, and such comfortable seats.

'They've been so good,' the stewardess said. 'How do you do it?'

I thought of what Barbara would do and said 'Perhaps someone could bring me the double-buggy, I think I can manage now'.

THE ENGINES OF OUR SPACESHIP

A piece of life writing, by Colin Gardiner

'Can we pretend we're in *Blake's Seven* again?' I ask Martin.

We are wasting another afternoon, sitting in the spare bedroom of Uncle Billy's house. The sun is beaming in through the net curtains, warm on our pale skinny arms. Tiny specks of dust float lazily in the air. There's a funny smell in the room. Martin says it's mothballs. They smell bad. We are surrounded by flowery wallpaper, yellow and pink. A cartoon jungle. A large double bed lies opposite the windows. We've been using the grey, itchy blanket as a battleground for our games.

I peep out through the net curtains and see the kids playing football in the street, screaming and laughing. They call us the Britser Boys. They laugh at the way we talk, but they let us play with them anyway. The street isn't too different to our own in Birmingham. They have little parks everywhere here in Dublin, with big statues of 'Our Lady' in them. Sometimes you see lines of cows being herded up the road at night.

I wanted us to join the kids outside, but Martin hates football. He puts down his Han Solo action figure and looks at me with his green-brown eyes. The same colour as mine.

'Only if you play the baddie.' Martin has his *Star Wars* t-shirt on. I like our Moscow Olympic t-shirts better. But Mom won't let us wear them here in Ireland, because they have Union Jacks on them.

'But the baddie is a woman,' I protest.

'Don't be a sexist.'

'What's a sexist?' I ask.

'It's a swear word. Like shit. Or bogies.' Martin is ten. Three years older than me. He knows a lot of swear words.

'I'm telling Uncle Billy!'

Uncle Billy is the eldest of our mother's brothers. He's not as tall as Superman, but he's quite big. His thick brown hair is always slicked back with cream. He's a serious man, but kind. He likes Martin and me, but he has a temper on him. He works as a glass blower and some of his creations lie around his house. The oval paperweight in the hallway. The large orange ashtray on the living-room coffee table. A gaping mouthed fish stands guard on the dressing table, staring at us. We know better than to touch it.

Martin ignores me and has moved over behind the door. 'Look over here.'

I crouch down and stare at the huge television set tucked into the corner. The plug is missing. An old fashioned telly. Unused. Martin pulls it out slowly across the rough carpet, which makes a purring sound. He removes the back. Inside six large glass tubes are lined up neatly on a green board with wires running everywhere. A fuzzy layer of dust coats everything.

'What are they?' I ask.

Martin carefully removes one of the tubes and holds it up to the sunlight. We see the tiny copper wires coiled up in weird patterns. Six small metal prongs stick out at the bottom of each tube. I press on one. It's sharp. Martin turns the object around slowly, throwing a swimming rainbow of colour onto the wall behind us.

'These are part of the engines. To our spaceship,' Martin murmurs as he shakes the tube slowly. It makes a faint tinkling noise. He hands it to me. 'You can be the engineer this time.'

'Smart!' I take the tube in my hands, my heart beating with excitement. 'What's an engineer?'

'Don't be so thick, for Christ's sake,' Martin snaps.

I notice the large picture of Jesus on the wall behind Martin. Christ (our Lord) is staring out at me with a cute lamb in his lap. He's sitting on a rock. Behind him are the lights of a small town. Martin turns around and sees the picture too.

'His eyes never stop looking at you,' he says quietly. 'It doesn't matter where you go.' To prove his point, Martin moves slowly around the room, eyes fixed on the picture.

'Stop it,' I cry. 'I'm scared.'

'Try it,' Martin replies.

I fix my gaze on the large blue eyes of the blond-haired Jesus. Without the beard, he almost looks like that blonde lady from Abba. I step sideways and bump into Martin.

'Watch out, you wally,' he shouts and shoves me.

'Feck off' I reply.

Martin grabs my arm. Frowning, he nods towards the picture of Jesus. 'Say "Sorry. Amen".'

'No.'

'Say it!' He squeezes my arm, harder.

'Sorry ... Amen.'

A small smashing noise startles us. We look down beside the bed. The broken tube lies on the floor. Gold wires and glass power. I hear a thump from downstairs and then the creaking of floor boards.

'What the feck is going on up there?' calls Uncle Billy.

'That's your fault,' hisses Martin, glaring at me and pointing at the mess.

The bedroom door swings open and there stands Uncle Billy, frowning, eyes wide. 'Can I not get a minute's peace with you two?' he growls. 'Which one of you did that?' He points to the broken glass.

I start to cry. I can't help it.

'Sorry, Uncle Billy. It was me,' Martin murmurs. He grabs my hand and squeezes it tight. I'm lucky I have a brother like him, to protect me.

I see my Aunt Kathleen standing behind Uncle Billy. She looks at Martin and me, concern in her eyes. A hastily tied headscarf hides her grey-brown hair. 'Ah Billy,' she says with a smile. 'Don't be giving them too much stick.' Aunt Kathleen is Uncle Billy's girlfriend. She's a kind woman and always laughing, although I don't think my Mom thinks too much of her.

'Stick?' snarls Uncle Billy. 'By Jesus, I'll show them some stick. I'll let their mother and father have it too, when they get back.'

Mom and Dad have gone out for the day to Bray to visit my Uncle Frank.

I start crying. 'Martin. Don't let them hit me with the stick,' I wail.

Aunt Kathleen leans down and puts her arm around me, laughing. 'Shhh. Don't be silly love,' she says.

I look at Martin. He rolls his eyes.

'Well, you can get the dustpan and clean that mess up,' Uncle Billy barks at Martin. 'Don't be bothering me again.'

A few days later and the breaking of the valve is forgotten. We are all crowded around the television in my Uncle Billy's living room.

Six kids watching *Top of the Pops*. It's early evening and the adults have gone to the club again. I press my nose against the cold window and sigh, turning the street lights into little halos. Martin is sitting on the sofa next to Mary, the girl from over the road.

Martin and Mary are both the same age and get on well. Martin plays with her, a lot more than he does with me. They are both laughing at Kate Bush dancing in the woods. She's in the top ten. I laugh too. Martin sits with both knees up to his chest. I pull my knees up and sit in the same position.

'Hey, Britser,' Eddy, Mary's older brother looks over at Martin, his mouth is somewhere between and smile and a sneer. 'Do you love the Queen?' Eddy is aged twelve. He's babysitting us. He has a big freckly face and a skinhead. I don't like him.

Martin looks up from the telly. 'Er. I don't know,' he says quietly.

Eddy snorts and nudges Mary. 'Hah. Do you hear him, Snotser? He doesn't know.' He stands up in front of the telly, arms crossed against his blue t-shirt. 'Well I bloody hate her.' He glares down at Martin. 'Do you hear me, Britser?'

'Eddy, leave him alone,' says Mary.

Eddy turns to his sister. 'Is he your boyfriend, Snotser? Is that it?' He reaches over and tugs at her hair.

'Ow!' Mary cries. 'Piss off.' She half-laughs and pushes at Eddy's arm.

Eddy slaps her face. Play-like at first. Mary laughs. And then he hits her again, harder. A fist. Straight in the face. A horrible thump that makes me feel sick.

'Stop it, Eddy. Stop it.' Mary screams, tears streaming down her face. Blood running from her nose.

Eddy keeps punching her.

Martin suddenly bolts up from the sofa, wide-eyed, breathing heavily. 'Stop,' he shouts. 'Stop hitting her.' His fists are clenched and his body is shaking.

Eddy swings around suddenly and steps up to Martin. He is about a head taller than my brother. His freckled face even redder than before. 'You want some too, Britser?' he screams, spit flying onto Martin's t-shirt. 'Because I'll give you some too, by Christ I will.'

My heart pounds quickly. Everyone in the room is looking at Martin, their mouths open. I sit up slowly from my seat and clench my fists too. 'Say sorry amen, bastard,' I whisper.

Eddy looks at me with his dead, blue eyes. He smiles and winks at me. He suddenly raises a fist at Martin. Martin steps back and falls back onto the sofa, head bent down. Mary gets up and leaves the room, quietly crying.

'And don't be thinking of telling on me this time, Snotster,' Eddy calls out to her. He looks back at us all and sneers. Then he reaches over and switches channel on the television. There's a football match on. He sits back in his chair and stretches his legs.

I reach into my pocket and pull out the valve. I run my finger across the six small metal prongs sticking out at the bottom. I jump up from my seat and scoot up next to Martin. I grab his hand and press the valve into his hand.

He turns to me, red faced.

'Don't be such a baby.'

Martin shoves the glass tube back at me. There's a small, tinkling noise. I pull back and glance down. The glass splinter leaves a bleeding cut on my finger.

SPRING EXPEDITION

A piece of fiction, by Lucie Glasgow

Malcolm had a Fiat Panda. I don't remember what reg it was but, although we probably all commented on it, I don't think any of us cared. It was black, which showed all the scratches, but it had two sunroofs which we thought was really cool. Also, none of the other village lads had a car, so none of its crappiness really mattered.

I don't know if it was the first sunny day in May, or it was just because it was a Sunday, but there was this one day when it just seemed wrong to stay at home. I was meant to be studying for my exams, but I was getting sick of it. I'd been spending day after day curled over my desk, looking at labelled diagrams of the parts of a beetle and the process of osmosis. I wasn't even sure it was getting in my head anymore.

I happened to looked out of my window and I saw Malcolm out on his driveway. Him and his dad were tinkering with the Fiat. When he saw me and waved I thought I'd use it as an excuse to get out of the house for a second, so I went out to say hello.

As I approached, Malcolm was sat in the car, revving the engine, while his dad stared under the opened bonnet.

'That's better,' his dad was shouting over the engine. 'It's sounding really good now. Smooth as a Roller.'

It sounded the same as it always did to me, but what did I know? Malcolm's dad seemed very impressed though, and began explaining enthusiastically to me how well each part of the engine was working, and how he'd got it to do so. I showed as much interest as I could, but I was relieved when he suggested that Malcolm and I took it out for a drive, to see how good it was.

When the car had reached the end of our street Malcolm turned left, onto the road leading out of the village.

'Where are we going?' I asked him.

'Don't know, Andy,' he answered. Then, with mock over-enthusiasm, he added 'We could go anywhere!'

'Anywhere?' I echoed, with the same manic tone. 'Even as far as Woolthorpe?' I suggested, as we entered the village of Woolthorpe.

'Even as far as Anwell.'

'Anwell?' That one was about two miles further. 'We could see if Dan's in.'

'We could,' said Malcolm. 'And Pete.'

About ten minutes later we were out on the road again, but now we had Dan and Pete in the back. When Pete had suggested that we went to a pub to enjoy a cold pint in a beer garden, it had sounded like the sort of thing we wanted to be normal for us to do. So we all said 'Yeah,' as if it was the most obvious action, and Pete added that The Swan back in Woolthorpe was good, so we headed for that.

The bar was busy when we got inside, and we had to wait to get served. We stood together in a tight group, like we were first years in big school, and I don't think we blended in nearly as well as we'd imagined we would. This was back when you could smoke in pubs, and in my first attempt at leaning casually on the bar my elbow landed in a well-used ashtray.

The landlord was this miserable guy my parents knew – I think his name was Bill West – and I could see him grunting at the customers at the other end of the bar. We got served by this younger bloke in a rugby shirt. I tried to imitate his nonchalance as I asked for three pints of Carling and a Coke.

None of us let on what a relief it was to have secured our drinks, as we navigated our way around chairs, tables and the odd dog, and out the back door. Pete marched across the sunny garden, and we followed him, leaving clumsy trails of drips from our turbulent glasses.

Once we were safely established at our selected picnic table, having managed to get all of our legs over the bench and under the table without looking too awkward, we passed smug looks around as conspiratorial congratulations. We were enjoying a drink in a pub garden on a sunny Sunday afternoon.

We were at the far corner of the garden, but only a low fence separated us from a steep, grassy bank that led down to the river. The water looked cool and inviting. It was shallow there, not much above ankle-deep, and there was a woman watching her two children have a paddle. It reminded me of something from an idyllic Victorian painting.

'Aren't there pike in that river?' said Pete.

'No,' scoffed Dan. 'Well, not there, anyway.'

'We'll soon see,' said Malcolm, 'if one of them kids gets pulled under.'

We all laughed.

'They're not that dangerous,' said Dan.

'Don't they bite?' I asked.

'Nah, it's a myth,' explained Dan. 'Well, they can. But they usually only bite you if you're trying to catch them.'

'Oh, so they hunt fishermen?' asked Pete.

We gave him a round of sarcastic laughter.

But the mood was quickly broken. The old boy from behind the bar – the one I think was called Bill West – he came over to our table. I just looked up and noticed him striding across the grass. His skin shone red through his white stubbly beard, as he marched straight up to us and started pointing at Dan.

'You,' he shouted, 'you. How old are you?'

Dan stammered, shocked, 'I, I'm . . .'

'You're not eighteen,' Bill informed him. 'You're not. I know you're not.'

'I am,' replied Dan, getting it together. 'I was eighteen in March.'

'Don't give me that.' Bill rested a trembling hand on the table and leant towards him. 'I know you. I know your mother.'

'I'm eighteen,' Dan pleaded.

'He is. He's eighteen,' added Malcolm, for good measure.

But it was no good now. Pete had started laughing. There'd been a snort, and then some suppressed giggling, but it wasn't very subtle and it set me off. Malcolm tried to ignore us but I even saw him smile.

'Right, out, all of you,' Bill demanded. His face was now near crimson. 'Go on. Get out.'

'What?' protested Dan, in disbelief.

'I mean it,' said the glowing Bill. 'I'm not having underage drinking here.'

We did all start to get up then. Pete tried to down his pint quickly but he was laughing too much and it made him choke. That got me going, and even Malcolm a bit, but it turned old Bill nearly purple.

'Put the drinks down and get out,' he yelled. I'd never actually seen someone wave their arms about in anger before. It made him look like dancing puppet.

'We're going,' answered Dan. He was the only one not laughing.

We made our exit through a gate in the fence, conveniently close to our bench. This was a stroke of genius on Malcolm's part, because it robbed Bill of the chance to frogmarch us back through the pub like unruly children. We had to go the long way round to get to the car park but it was worth it.

We tried to think of some other pub to go to but none of us knew which ones would serve us, and Dan was convinced that he wouldn't get served in any. In the end we decided to just try to get some beers from somewhere and find a nice spot to sit and drink them. It felt a bit like defeat, but at least we weren't heading home. Just round the corner from The Swan there was a shop with some parking spaces nearby, so we left the car there and Pete went in for some cans. The rest of us waited outside, nervously.

Woolthorpe wasn't a village that we hung round much so we struggled to think of a place to go. We didn't want to go to the rec because that was a known spot for underage drinking, so the only other place we could think of was the river.

'But it's right next to the pub,' Dan protested. 'What if that guy comes after us?'

'It's not his land,' said Pete. 'Nothing he can do.'

Dan didn't look convinced.

'He's not gonna care,' I reassured him. 'He probably won't see us, anyway. He'll be busy enough in the bar.'

Dan seemed a bit less worried by the time we got as far as the pub. Pete seemed determined to turn the whole thing into some sort of secret mission. I wasn't sure if he was trying to cheer Dan up or to frighten him, but it seemed to do a bit of both. Anyway, he did this exaggerated, comedy, creeping walk as we went down the side of the pub and it made us laugh so we all joined in. When he got to the beginning of the fence that surrounded the garden he ducked down, and we copied that as well. It would have made us more conspicuous but by that stage we didn't care. When he reached the end of the garden, he opened the gate and walked in.

'What are you doing?' I asked, in an exaggerated whisper. There wasn't anyone down that end of the garden but I'd got into the charade.

'Grab the other end,' he said, matter-of-factly. He took a hold of the picnic bench we'd been sat at before, and lifted it slightly.

'What?' I protested, but Malcolm found it funny.

'Pete, you can't,' he told him, but he was laughing.

'Come on,' said Pete, sounding more urgent. 'Quick, or the angry man will see.'

Before any of us - – well, certainly me anyway - – knew what was happening, we were all helping to lift the thing over the gateway. It was heavy and awkward, and I'm not sure how we managed it, but one thing I do remember is that we were all laughing, mainly because we were terrified. As soon as it was over, we each grabbed a corner and instinctively started to run, or something like it. We couldn't go very fast. The thing was such a clumsy shape, and it was difficult to manoeuvre on the slope.

'Where are we going?' asked Malcolm.

'To have a drink by the river,' answered Pete in his isn't-it-obvious tone.

Fortunately, there was no-one else by the river then. I don't know what they'd've made of four lads carrying a picnic bench if there had been. We didn't know what to make of it, and when we stopped we all turned to Pete to see if he was going to give us an explanation. He stood with his hands on his hips for a moment, surveying the scene. Then he pulled off his trainers and started rolling up the bottoms of his jeans.

'What are we doing now?' asked Dan.

'Gentlemen,' said Pete, still folded double, 'in order to experience the cooling effect of the water, one must be in it.'

I had no idea what he meant at that stage, but it wouldn't have made sense to back out then, so I copied Pete, and so did the others. It clicked when he lifted up one end of the table again, and asked Dan to bring the beers.

There was a brief moment where I thought that Pete had had the best idea in the world. Sitting at a picnic bench on a hot day with a cold lager, our feet being cooled by the river water, seemed perfect. The table legs did sink a bit into the soft silt, and more on mine and Pete's side than Malcolm and Dan's, but we just adjusted ourselves to the slant and opened our beers. Malcolm opened his Coke can and held it up.

'To ingenuity,' he said, 'and to freedom. Cheers.'

Me and Dan both gave a hearty 'Cheers' in reply. But Pete looked distracted.

'Er, Pete?' prompted Dan.

Pete squinted at something in the distance before turning to us. 'To getting the fuck out of here,' he announced. 'Run!'

He took a swig from his can as he swung his legs out of the

bench. I looked up and saw Bill West running down the hill towards us, his arms flapping like alternating paddles at his sides. The rest of us followed Pete back to the bank where we grabbed our shoes. Then we ran off along the river, with Bill huffing and puffing along behind. Fortunately, he wasn't as fast as he was angry, and we managed to make it across a footbridge and behind a large hedge before he could see where we'd gone.

Or he may have given up. But we were pretty rattled by then and we stayed absolutely still, pressing ourselves into the hedge, for what seemed like hours, before we felt brave enough to bend down and put our trainers back on. We didn't dare go back the way we'd come, so we walked a really long route all round the village to get to the car. By the time we reached it all conversation had stopped. I had half expected to find it smashed to bits, or for Bill to be there waiting for us, and I think it was the same with the others too. We climbed inside as quickly and quietly as we could, and I can't tell you how much of a relief it was when we drove past the last house and were clear of the village.

When we were sure we'd got out, Dan broke the silence by saying 'Do you think that man will've called the police?'

We all thought about it for a moment.

'What's he gonna tell them if he does?' Malcolm pointed out. 'We didn't do any real damage. Not really.'

'Hmmm,' said Dan, unconvinced.

'Don't forget he knows you're underage', I pointed out. 'If he reports us he'll have to admit that one of his staff served and underage drinker.'

'That's true,' Malcolm agreed.

'And it's not like we broke the bench,' added Pete. 'We just moved it. So what? It's a moveable bench.' He drummed his fingers on the back of Malcolm's seat. 'If he doesn't want his furniture moved he should nail it down.'

He said it with a straight face, so we all sort of nodded in agreement. I don't know if he saw me and Malcolm smirking at each other in the front. I'm glad we didn't laugh out loud, 'cos Dan was still sitting there looking very shaken up.

'Guys,' he said after a long pause, 'we don't tell anyone about this, yeah?'

A furtive look was passed around. Malcolm flicked on the indicator as the car readied to turn into Anwell.

And we all agreed.

THE TRUTH IN MASQUERADE

A work of fiction, by Ruth F Hunt

'Jesus, Mick, why peg it now?'

I stood facing the shit-coloured lumpy settee, wit' all the cushions bunched up into one corner. I could imagine him lyin' there, can in one hand, remote in the other. I felt like salutin' (not that I ever was in the forces).

On the mantelpiece was a nearly bald string o' blue tinsel pinned in place by empty bottles of whisky, cans an' towering ashtrays.

Shaking me head I muttered: 'Tinsel in fuckin' April!'

Through a tear in the grimy nets, there was like this tunnel of light showin' up all the crap in the air. It pointed towards the right side of the settee where I spotted a tiny white triangle pokin' out. I got me biro from behind me ear and tugged on it, pullin' out a creased an' stained photo.

It was Mick around my age, late 50s, maybe a bit older. Balanced o' his knee was a little girl wit' her white-blonde hair scraped up into wonky bunches. She looked like she'd got right gob on her.

It kicked off memories of our Sally. I could feel me hand stingin' after I'd whacked her across her face. A few minutes later she legged it, slammin' the front door so hard the whole house shook. Since then, nott'n, not even a friggin' word.

The coppa stuck his head around the door.

'Are you ready?'

'Yer seen this?' I pointed down at the photo.

He joined me and nosed at it, his hands gripped behind his back.

'I'm thinkin' it might be a niece?'

'DC Owens and his team will be doing a full search tomorrow.'

'Why, if yer reckon it was a heart attack or summat like that?'

'It's just procedure, Mr Turner. Are you ready?'

I followed him out and watched as he pushed his belly forward and arched his back, like the daffodils behind him breakin' free of the soil.

'It's going to take a fair bit of work getting it ready for your next tenant.'

'Yer tellin me. I've had nott'n but bad luck wit' this place. First there was this girl who robbed us, then the floodin ...'

'Ah yes, this was one of the flooded roads.'

'For four friggin' months. At first I thought it wasn't goin' to be that bad, but when all the water had gone there were loads o' damage to put right. Mick was me first tenant after that an' the best one by miles.'

'Was he?'

'Easy. Yer don't need us now, do yer?'

'No, you're free to go.'

I made me way back to me car an' transferred the carrier bag wit' the chippy papers into the wheelie bin on the pavement while nobody was watchin'. I pulled me seatbelt over me belly an' for a second stretched both arms over the steering wheel, me head in between 'em. It didn't seem right; a war hero like Mick bundled away, wit' no fuss.

I sat back up an' noticed DC Owens was back.

'Bloody pufter.'

When I first turned up at number 24 after gettin' the phone call from the bizzies, I was about to make me way up the path when DC Owens put his arm around me back an' moved me to the side of the pavement. There he was in a crumpled suit, floppy hair an' by God was he lookin' down at me.

He raised his eyebrows: 'When was the last time you saw Mick?'

'Now yer talkin'. God, I don't know, a year, maybe?'

'He wasn't a friend of yours?'

'I told yer – I'm his landlord.'

'I know you're his landlord but I'm wondering why you let him rent the property? I'm assuming you took up references, did checks?'

'Course. Anyhow, Mick isn't just some old git. He was in the navy. A friggin' war hero.'

Wit' his hands on his hips the detective glanced at St Christopher's.

'Must be popular this road.' He raised an eyebrow: 'What with the primary school being so near?'

'Well, that's just statin' the bleedin' obvious, isn't it?'

The detective shared a look wit' the coppa.

'What?'

'Nothing, Sir. Nothing at all.'

The coppa tapped the detectives arm and pointed to me. Wit' a flick of his hair, DC Owens glanced up from his phone and across at me.

'Alright, alright, give us a chance.'

I pulled out of the parking space, and revved the engine as I passed them. No wonder the council tax bills were so bleedin' high if they investigated every bloody death.

Back at ours, I got out a can o' Stella from the fridge an' raised it up a silent toast to Mick. I'm sure most landlords wouldn't have even let him in their office, let alone anythin' else. He was like a tramp wit' mucky clothes, bogeys hangin' from his nose, an' he smelt like a mixture o' sweaty socks an' Scotch. What drew me to him was the loneliness. I could see it in his eyes. Summat I knew all too well.

'Yer haven't filled in the next o' kin question,' I said, when Mick returned the rental agreement.

Wit' his face blank showin' no emotion, he stared at me blinkin' slowly, his eyes dark and heavy-lidded.

'Active service changed me.' He stuck his elbows on the desk, his head in his hands.

'It'd change anyone, mate.'

He began to pick at a grubby wart on one of his fingers: 'I'm not a nice man, not nice at all, and with the PTSD and all that.'

I banged me fist down on me desk: 'You're a bloody hero and don't you forget it.'

It was a week after his death and I was still waitin' for the 'ok' from DC Owens that I could start emptyin' the property. I'd just nipped to Tesco an' was loadin' up me freezer wit' microwave meals, when I heard a car pull up o' the gravel drive.

I opened the door to a dead flustered DC Owens who was rakin' his long fingers through his hair.

'Just to update you – you'll be able to access your property in the next few days. Sorry it's taken so long.'

'What about his funeral? Who arranges that?'

DC Owens batted me question away wit' his hand: 'He was cremated. The council sorted that out.'

'Shit, I wanted to go.'

'Really?' DC Owens shook his head: 'It was just a cremation, no service.'

'That doesn't seem right. He should have a service, like a memorial or summat like that?'

The detective wagged his finger at me: 'Be very careful, his past was unsavoury to say the least.'

'Oh, he told us all about that.'

DC Owens raised an eyebrow: 'And you still want a service?'

'Course. Better than how he's bin treated, like some … some … Like some dirty secret.'

His nostrils flared: 'I don't know how you can stand there and say that. I really don't.'

'That makes bloody two of us then.' I banged the door shut, and stuck me middle finger up.

That fuckin' detective sayin' that meant I had to arrange summat, even if just to spite him. The only church I knew was St Christopher's in the centre o' the village, so I decided to walk it, an' get some fresh air.

When we first moved from Liverpool to Lancashire, we thought we were goin' up in the world. Me, Sheila an' our Sally. Wit' just me left, I felt out o' place. As for Westonville, it might look alright, wit' the stone terraced housin' an' dead pricey barn conversions, but I realised it was a shithole just like anywhere else.

I staggered into the grounds o' the church, sweatin' and for a second leant against the railings and planted me hands o' me knees tryin' to catch me breath.

'Are you ok?' A grey-haired lady said, her hand restin' on me back.

I straightened up, and wiped me face wit' me hand.

'Fine, thanks love.'

She clutched a battered Bible wit' pages marked by loads o' multicoloured post-it notes.

'Are you the ... I thought it was some fella?'

'He's leading the worship in a church in Dorset.'

'And yer a proper vicar, like?'

She stood with her legs wide apart: 'Indeed, despite only being a woman.'

'Yer might be able to help us then. Me tenant Mick has peg ... I mean he's died. He was in his 80s an' a war-hero. Could you do us a service for' him?'

'A funeral service?'

'Nah, he's bin cremated already. I mean like a memorial service.'

'Was he a churchgoer?'

I shook me head: 'Is that a problem?'

'It is. If he was a regular here I might've been able to squeeze him in on a Sund–'

I interrupted her: 'I was wantin' to raise some money for Help for Heroes.'

'What about a Just Giving page? You can share it on Facebook.'

'I've never done nott'n like that before.'

'Look up "Just Giving" on Google and follow the instructions. It isn't hard.'

It took us two friggin' days to set up Facebook, an' a Just Giving page. They wanted us to put summat about why people should donate. So I wrote some bullshit, most of it guesswork.

I shared the Just Giving Page. Nott'n happened and I thought me £1,000 target was a bit o' a stretch. Then a goalie for Westonville Town F.C. shared it an after that it was like fuckin' magic.

One fella arrived at me door wit' his wife. He had this white shirt on so tight could see his tats under it. His rectangular haircut, wit' shaved sides wobbled as he spoke.

'So which wars did Mick fight in?'

'I'm not exactly … He had that PTSD thing, didn't like talkin' 'bout it.'

'Lots of cowboys around making out they're ex-forces.'

'Mick wasn't one of 'em. Think he saw stuff …' I scratched behind me ear: 'Stuff he couldn't forget.'

His wife sighed: 'Just give him the cheque.'

'I have a special place just here,' he patted the top right o' his chest, 'for all those who served this country.' He took a step forward and handed me the white envelope.

'Me too. Mick an' heroes like him.'

I totted up everythin' that afternoon. It was only £173.40 off the target so I put that in meself and announced the target had bin reached. I posted Help for Heroes tellin' 'em about the money raised and Mick, I found meeself nearly in tears.

'Yer daft old sod.'

The only pain in the arse was Help for Heroes didn't reply, which pissed me right off.

STORIES FROM EVERYWHERE – AN ANTHOLOGY

A few days later, I finally could get in number 24. I called up me mate Bill an his two teenage lads to help us empty the property before it could be swilled over wit' some bleach and a slap o' paint where it needed it.

After a long day, I parked up in me drive and opened the door. Suddenly, I saw a dark shape. I was dragged out by me jacket and slammed against the back door of me car.

'What the … ?'

It was the guy wit' the block haircut, his face purple wit' thick blood vessels in his neck throbbin'. His tattooed left hand was in a massive fist an' dead close to me nose. I felt the flask of milky coffee I'd slurped down at number 24 sloshin' around me bladder an' a tight feelin' of pressure, before a burnin' trickle ran down me right leg.

'You fucking scouse pervert. You got me and my Elaine to give money to that … that fucking monster. You must have some twisted fucked-up mind to think he was a hero.'

'Wha … ?'

His fist moved closer to us nose, and then blurred out of shape. The trickle of piss was now a puddle by me foot.

He sniffed and looked down, raisin' up his knees to get his feet out o' the way. As he did, his grip loosened. I squirmed free, and legged it into me house. As I put the chain on, he started to go mental, yellin' an' bootin' the door.

The phone in the hallway rang.

A woman chanted: 'Friend of a paedo. Friend of a paedo.'

'What the hell's goin' on?'

'Look at Facebook.' The phone went dead.

I ran upstairs and spread a towel over me bed, me kecks now soakin'. It seemed to take friggin' ages to log onto Facebook.

The first message I saw was from Help for Heroes:

'Thank you for the money collected but Michael Henson was never in the forces.

http://www.newsfornorthwest/waltermittypaedophilejailed.com'

I clicked the link, and as a read the report I felt as though I was drownin'. I gripped the bed as me stomach churned, wit' sick floodin' me mouth. I staggered into the bathroom, me chest tight an' shootin' pains up an' down me arms. The tiled floor seemed to be swayin'. I felt dead dizzy, an' collapsed between the bog an' bath.

He'd got nine years for the abuse of a girl from the age of 6 to 10 and havin' kiddie porn. They said he was a 'Walter Mitty' character who tried to hide who he really was wit' this naval officer crap.

Mick had probably scouted around until he found summat close to kids. Then, instead of the usual checks and reference taking, he found a dickhead of a landlord who believed every fuckin' lie he trotted out, no questions asked.

'Shit, what've I done?'

I cleaned meself up, an' closed all me curtains, hidin' in bed.

Sit tight, Bill said. So that's what I did, but there's only so much Jeremy friggin' Kyle you can take. After a week, I wanted to risk it, start facin' the world again.

I didn't have long to wait, cos just after 7am I woke up wit' an engine runnin' outside me house.

I stood at the side of the window and pulled open me curtains at the side.

Down below, a taxi driver was helpin' some woman out. She glanced up to me window.

'Bloody hell, Sally?'

I threw me dressing gown on an' stumbled downstairs, me feet goin' too fast for me body. Summat wasn't right, though, she hadn't knocked on the door. I opened up just to see the arse end of her climbin' back in the taxi.

'Sally!' I started to run, but the taxi screeched off.

As I turned back round I saw that on me mat was a copy of The Courier wit' a red ribbon round it.

I shoved some crap off me kitchen table before unwrappin' an' spreadin' it out.

The front page was goin' on 'bout the new flood defences gettin' the go-ahead. Was that what she wanted me to see?

I made some coffee, an' flicked through. There on page 9 was a massive photo o' me, wit' the headline, 'Daughter Speaks Out.'

As I tried to read the first line, where she said I'd physically abused her as a kid by breakin' her jaw at 16, a shootin' pain in me ribs took me breath away.

I gasped: 'Jesus, Sally, why now?'

Wit' all me strength I lobbed me coffee cup at the wall, an' let out this roar that turned into a whimper. Pain in me chest and neck was makin' the newsprint look blurry. I tried to get a drink o'water but as soon as I stood up, the kitchen turned on its side and I was thrown backwards, hittin' me head on the cooker. That's when everythin' went black.

RETURN OF THE LADYBIRD

A work of fiction, by Katya Karnachova

The door banged open and Ari skidded into the room. 'They're here!' He breathed out.

Curled up in a plush chair, Jerica looked up from the book. Ari was doubled over, hands on knees, gasping loudly to catch his breath. His grin fell when she only cocked her head at his news. Still panting, he strode up, took her hand into his sweaty own and pulled her out of the chair.

'Come on! We waited ...so long ... for this.' Ari took a deep breath to steady his voice. 'You waited so long for this.'

Jerica felt her cheeks catch fire. She yanked her hand from Ari's.

'I'm OK. I mean –' Jerica shook her head to clear it. 'I'd rather give them space. They've been through so much.'

'He'll be pissed off if he doesn't see you in the crowd.'

Jerica snorted. Ari sounded a lot like his brother despite being separated from him for four years. Something caught in her throat as it made a mad dash for freedom. She made a soft sound somewhere between a choke and a groan. How could Riley up and leave her like that?

'Come on,' Ari said softly, outstretching his hand to Jerica again.

She ignored it. A sudden desire to see Riley took over, moving her body automatically out of the house.

She joined the stream of latecomers flowing towards the docks and with single-minded determination pushed people out of her way. Concern momentarily flared at the back of her mind that she didn't lock the front door, but quenched it with the knowledge that Ari would do it.

Half a mile away from the docks it became impossible to move. Everyone was so closely packed together not even a knife would fit between them. Bright bunting hung on every street among bright flowers, waving in the breeze, catching the sunshine and reflecting the colours onto the white houses. Excitement radiated from everyone, pushing against Jerica, penetrating into her every fibre. Now she couldn't believe she didn't want to come here.

Over the babble of talk, yells, and laughter, Jerica made out a thin thrill of a whistle. Looking up at the roofs she spotted Ari on one of them. They locked eyes for a moment and both nodded in silent understanding. Scanning her surroundings, she found a wide back topped by a set of very sturdy shoulders a little further ahead. Ignoring the annoying grunts coming from those past whom she forced her way through, Jerica grabbed the back of the man's tunic and scaled him with an ease of an alley cat.

'Hey, Mark,' she said, ruffling the butcher's hair.

'Huh,' he grunted in reply, unsurprised and unperturbed of having a passenger perched on his shoulders.

'Think you can take me closer to a building? Any side will do.'

'Uh-huh.'

A ripple of displeasure emanated from the crowd as Mark made a beeline for the houses, but anyone voicing their anger stopped the moment they saw who pushed them. Being a mute of considerable size who was good with a cleaver definitely had perks. Within moments, Jerica was close enough to a building to hop onto its balcony on the first floor.

'Thanks!' She waved at Mark without looking at him.

Once on a roof, she looked on the other side of the street, noticing Ari give her a quick wave before dashing off towards the pier.

'Race ya!'

At least that's what she thought he yelled at her. His voice was lost in the roar of the crowd and got carried away by the breeze. Jerica accepted the challenge and didn't wait to start covering the distance between them. An inner child surfaced, and with pure glee she hopped, ran, and skid along the red tiles. Her troubles fled and her problems were gone, vaporised in the warm sun shining down from the cloudless skies. Just like that she was back to being fourteen years old again, that carefree kid with so much love to give and wonder to be quenched.

The buildings parted, letting the perfection of a horseshoe-shaped landing dock unfold itself like a picture from a pop-up book. The view of the colourless flat expanse usually littered with smaller aircrafts like racers, bigger fish like cargo haulers, and an occasional frigate-like monstrosity bristled with weapons took her breath away every time. Today, however, the sight slammed the air out of her lungs with a force of weapon master's hammer.

It was four days ago that Ladybird first made contact with the Gallanian authorities, flying back to Purto non-stop ever since. Having that long to mentally get ready for the vessel to be there in all her glory, Jerica learned right there and then that in reality, she wasn't prepared in the slightest. At first glance, Ladybird looked like she did four years ago on the day of her departure, but Jerica could pick out the damage. Multiple dents of various sizes peppered Ladybird's body, its rear end blackened as if licked by flame of immense heat. Whatever colours were present at the beginning of the voyage have long faded.

Ari cursed under his breath but Jerica was too preoccupied with drinking in the sight of every speck of damage visible that she didn't bother to scold him. She wasn't even surprised that he appeared by her side so quickly. Then Ari hissed through gritted teeth, like he always did when he got himself bitten by one of the street cats. Wondering what has caused him pain this time, Jerica took her eyes off Ladybird to look at him but instead her gaze fell upon the crew.

No. The group wasn't the crew. They were fathers gathered together to greet their sons back home. But they were too thin and too dark to be fathers. In comparison to the locals gathered round, they were like flakes of volcanic ash scattered on a golden sandy beach. One of the old men looked up, scanning the rooftops, as if looking for something, knowing it would be up there.

A sudden hot flush filled Jerica's mouth with cotton wool and made her hands too damp to have any grip on the tiles. She started sliding off the roof and her movement caused the man to hone in on her. For a moment their eyes locked, and that same instant she knew. No one else had those eyes. She let out a strangled cry before she lost her grip and plummeted towards the ground.

'Stop pestering me, I'm fine!'

Jerica beat the medic's hands away for the umpteenth time. She was angry at herself for losing her grip. No, not angry. She was fuming, and ready to breathe fire at anyone in the vicinity, which did include the medic who could give Mark a good run for his

STORIES FROM EVERYWHERE – AN ANTHOLOGY

money at being the biggest man in town.

But she was also scared. Terrified for what she saw from the rooftop, the cause of her fall that was cushioned by the people milling about underneath. She tried to get someone to persuade the Fleet Admiral to talk to her and let her see the crew, to see Riley, but hours later she was still waiting. Maybe if the Fleet Admiral was to come in right that moment and personally refuse her, she could spit-roast him with her anger. Yup, that would be nice. The old man was overdue a date with death anyway.

'Alright, Miss Smarty Pants.' The medic indicated the door with his head. 'Dismissed.'

The sound of metallic clinking of medical equipment followed Jerica as she scampered out of the medic's house onto sunlit emptying streets. Now that Ladybird had been moved into a hangar and her crew taken to the Town Hall, people started going back to their normal lives. A large number still mulled about, some sitting at the outdoor tables of different cafés, others looking down from friends' balconies with drinks in their hands.

'Life's good when it's the weekend.'

Ari leaned against the medic's house with his eyes half closed. His new outfit matched Jerica's down to a fibre.

'Life's better when I know the answers.'

Ari snorted in reply.

'You can know the answers. The Fleet Admiral was called in for an emergency meeting.'

Jerica raised an eyebrow to show she understood the hint. However, Ari pretended to be busy checking his nails for cracks and dirt. It was time to appeal to his ego.

'You being so clever and all ...' Jerica trailed off.

'Carry on,' Ari purred.

'Would you happen to know how to get into his house without any problems?'

Ari looked into her eyes, a malicious grin spreading wide on his face.

Jerica was propped against the closed door, looking at the large garden sprawled in front of her. People sat behind the table, all talking, most drinking, few eating. No one paid her any attention. For a while she stood there, torn between going back through the door or approaching the crowd. Time was short, as the Fleet Admiral could be back at any moment. Ari had posted himself on the roofs, ready to let out three shrill yells like a seagull in case Jerica had to make a quick and unseen getaway.

Taking a deep breath to steady her nerves, Jerica took one step towards the table. Riley looked up, locking his eyes with hers, and her body seized up. With growing terror, she watched him excuse himself from the table and approach her. A number of his crew kept an eye on him, but most didn't bother breaking their conversations. With every step he took closer, her heartbeat increased until it galloped against her ribs. When Riley was just few feet away, without thinking and breaking the eye contact, Jerica pushed against the door that instantly gave in under her weight. She took a few steps back, immersing herself into the cool shadow of the building. For a moment he was framed in the doorway, a solid black outline of a man silhouetted against bright day. But then he moved in and closed the door.

'Hey,' he whispered.

Her eyes got used to the darker interior, colours became

brighter, and for the first time she had a proper look at her ex. He should have been twenty-six now, and there should still be only two years between them. But the man standing in front of Jerica looked old enough to be her grandfather. Still a head taller, his hair gathered in a ponytail, once blacker than coal, was now as white as the building they were in. The face she remembered as being smooth and carefree was now framed with a beard and covered with scars and wrinkles. His beige tunic and matching pants seemed far paler against his tanned skin than they would have done on her. Even his eyes have lost that magical sparkle.

Her hands were surprisingly steady when she reached out and cupped his face.

'What happened?' Jerica asked, feeling burning at the back of her eyes.

Riley shook his head.

'We went through some sort of portal. It took us forever to find the way back.'

'You mean a portal to another world?'

Instead of answering, he took her hands in his and kissed them. They stood a while like that, not saying a word.

The three seagull calls brought Jerica back with a flush of panic.

'I have to go,' she said, urgency making her voice quiver. 'I'll see you later. I promise.'

And with that she freed herself from Riley's gentle grip and run through the corridors that would take her to the side door used by the Fleet Admiral's staff.

Tears spilled as she ran, passing people, ignoring their calls to her. She always imagined everything falling into place with Riley's return, as if the long separation never happened. She always imagined spending the rest of her life with him. Instead, he had aged at a far greater rate than she expected.

At least she got part of what she wished for.

At least she has seen him reach his old age.

NAVAGIO BEACH

A poem, by Megane Kilpatrick

There's no Navajos here on Navagio beach,
just mermaids and pirates who will besiege
a shipwrecked cove full of mystery.
I have donned a silky swimsuit livery
ready for a barbarous battle to the death
but first I must lie, relax and catch my breath.
A layer of oil to marinate myself in the sun
then a slow bake for two hours at a lavish thirty one.
I am savouring this heavenly cliché slice
of beach, the sashaying sea my only vice.
Craggy cliffs surround the sandy nook
the rusty boat has plenty space for a captain with a hook.
I flee to the sea as anchors are lifted
and sail through the water like a mermaid gifted
with poise and grace and Ariel-like hair.
The crystal clear view from underneath is rare,
I feel blessed to glimpse this aquatic haven
swimming with caretta caretta at the blue caves in
a sea so blue it could turn Uranus green.
Ancient ruins marbling the floor are fit for a queen,
remnants of a Zakynthos long lost to Poseidon
and the beached boat a relic sacrificed by a siren.
Floating on the surf like human silt
entranced by the ocean's beautiful lilt.

Gently gripping my toes into the delicate sand
wondering if I ever need to leave this enchanting land.

THE ROAD HOME

A work of fiction, by Carolien Kratz

'It's outrageous,' Ema had cried on hearing her father's news that the family was moving immediately to the new territories. 'You cannot expect me to move now, just as it's getting back to normal here. Besides, I've got an invitation to coffee tomorrow, and there's a dance at the regiment house on Saturday night. It's not fair.'

'Come now, Emlein,' her father had said, 'It's not as if you haven't been to hundreds of these parties and in time there will be more. But now, we have to bow to greater forces than our own desires. The victory is almost ours and we must play our part in it. Can you not understand this as an honour for us?'

'An honour? How can you think of honour? How can you expect us to just pack up and leave Mama and the baby? Did you ever think of that?'

Ema immediately regretted her words. It could not be easy for Papa either.

In the first days, before Mama and the tiny, partly-born brother had been buried, she had heard wretched howls from her father's bedroom late at night. But it had not been long before he returned to work with even more intensity than before. Did he still feel, after these few years, that deep anguish, that pain, which became so intense that she sometimes felt like running to the bridge over the river and throwing herself off it to release herself from it?

Some days she awoke after dreaming of her mother, simple dreams of her baking in the kitchen, putting away treasures in her bedside table drawer, arranging scented lilacs in the hallway; unremarkable memories that would suddenly stab her so precisely in the heart that she would double up in bed with agony, weeping tears that her mother would never wipe away. Other days, it would take several minutes before the desolation returned.

Sometimes, before Papa returned to the house, Ema would creep into his bedroom and open the drawers on the side where her mother used to sleep. Inside, mementos of their infancy, small curls of fine hair and silver boxes filled with milk teeth, helped to calm her. A small collection of photographs invariably showed her mother smiling a bit too brightly at the camera but they helped her to fix the details of her mother's face exactly. More and more it felt as if the recollection of her mother's face was moving further away, beyond her grasp.

Papa turned away. 'Emlein, we have to put away our personal sorrows. We are not abandoning Mama and the little one, they will lie with our forebears and I – and in time you and Otto too – will join them. But for now, we have greater responsibilities. An ancient enemy is on the run, we have to take the tide and secure our glorious victory. Can you do that? For Mama?'

'The ancient enemy be damned.' This time Ema's riposte was silent. Papa in this mood, calling on the authority of the state, reminded her of the old Papa, unassailable, stubborn and unconquerable. It was infuriating yet also comforting.

'We leave in two days. Gerlinde will help you pack. But Ema, we are not going to a place with coffee parties and dancing. That will come, I am sure, but for now you will need your practical things, sturdy things; one suitcase maximum.'

'But where will we stay? Do they have hotels there? Surely the war ...'

'The capital has been spared destruction, mainly because they chose not to engage, they ran like cowards. We will be given one of their houses.'

'Live in one of their houses? Surely you can't mean that, Papa. It's one thing to leave everything I have ever known, but do you think Mama would want me to be made to live in a sty inhabited by that scum?'

'Come, now, Emlein. Your mother would have accepted her part in our mission. You will too, or you are no daughter of ours. Our boys are cleaning up and by the time we arrive, we will have a blank slate. It's zero hour, time to rebuild the reclaimed territories.'

Ema spent the next two days shifting piles of clothing and objects from her armchair to the table and onto the bed. One suitcase, only one to take away the whole of her life; Papa was impossible.

'I can't do this, Linde,' she had called out on the second day. 'You used to live there, you tell me what to take with us.'

'Your father said one piece, Emlein,' the housekeeper remarked, 'you don't need to take all your mother's photographs, just take your favourite.   And whatever do you need these cups and plates for? They will have enough at the new house.'

'Maybe so, but I'm not going to use the same things those filthy pigs drink out of. And don't look at me like that,' she said peevishly. Guilt at the thoughtless way she had expressed herself magnified her anger.

Gerlinde took a step back and seemed to gather herself together.

'I don't know how to look at you, Miss Ema,' she said in a brittle voice.

'Well, it shouldn't be that much of a shock to you, Gerlinde. You know what they say about them.'

'Well, what do they say? More important, what do you say to me, knowing me as you do?'

'Don't be like that, Lindi, you know that none of us thinks you are like them anymore.'

'Anymore! Miss Ema, I am sorry but you cannot speak to me like that. What of the child who used to climb into my arms, the girl who needed her nurse to brush her hair over and over again, until the hurt of her loss became better?   And all the time you were just thinking "She's not like them"?'

'Sorry Lindi. I don't know what came over me. It's not knowing what's going to happen. The sadness. I am really sorry. Forgive me?'

'Forgive, yes. Forget? Not yet.'

They arrived at the new house in the early afternoon after a long, hot journey that had begun in the cool of that day's dawn. It was a beautiful summer day as the small group made their way into the newly liberated zone. Never before had the light seemed so bright, the sky so high and the countryside so vast.

For the last hours, the roads had been surprisingly empty, so they had made good progress. Tattered remnants of clothing and single shoes festooned the verges, speaking of great multitudes who had recently passed by.

The occupiers had long passed back through their front lines, Papa said. 'They tried to take their whole lives back with them, crazy fools.'

'The fewer of them that remain, the fewer enemies we will have,' Ema said.

Their abandoned cattle roamed the countryside in search of water and someone to take their milk. Several had already fallen prey to hungry soldiers.

'Our boys will have fine pickings,' the aide-de-camp rejoiced.

Coming on occasion into the small villages they would see dogs skulking in barns, and while smoke from stacks and chimneys no longer rose, light tremors echoing distant detonations and the unmistakable smell of burning signalled continued fighting in the west.

At last they had come into the town and pulled up outside a pleasant looking villa. Their arrival aroused a grey cat sleeping on the front porch, which stretched warily and then patted up to watch them climb down.

Inside, things were in reasonable order. Ema glanced about apprehensively, but there was nothing at which even a child would hesitate to look. It was reasonably clean – had the soldiers cleaned up for their arrival? The hallway smelt of dust but not polish. Passing into the kitchen, she suddenly felt like a visitor in someone else's life.

They had left tins of spices and a wooden box with salt in their dresser, rows of bottled fruit and ceramic pots with preserved meats lined the pantry shelves. They had left the curtains, the pictures on their walls. In the drawers, old receipts, photographs of people in fancy outfits and letters and on the shelves some books that no one could read because that world had gone. Upstairs, there were unfamiliar smells in the bathroom and the bedrooms, mainly coming from the drawers. These were the scents of a well-cared for house, definitely not the dirty smells Ema had been expecting.

While Papa supervised the unloading, the two women took out

STORIES FROM EVERYWHERE – AN ANTHOLOGY

fine linens from the drawers and examined the items. These were strange and foreign clothes, made from unfamiliar fabrics. Ema was surprised at the quality. They put on some of the items, stood in front of the mirror and automatically put their hands into pockets and found knotted handkerchiefs, old sweet wrappers and foreign coins. In the bedroom cabinet drawers they found envelopes out of which spilled milk teeth and small locks of carefully wrapped hair. Ema felt her heart open. These precious remnants did not deserve to be thrown out. She would become their guardian.

After a somewhat improvised supper prepared by the aide-de-camp and Gerlinde, Ema went up to bed in the main bedroom. From her luggage she withdrew the favourite photograph she had selected to bring with her, she changed into her night clothes, covered herself with one of the coats and fell asleep on the bed closest to the cabinet. She had come home.

92

ABERFAN

A piece of life writing, by Beverley Lucas

The woman behind the counter glares when I tell her there was no need to have closed the cafe: this is them open for business. Megabytes on Aberfan Road have been in business 20 years. Initially opened as a venue for homework clubs and computer lessons, the growing popularity of home broadband has seen a marked decline in the need for its facilities. But with only one other person here, Hettie isn't difficult to find.

Hettie's hair is grey, and her face lined. She looks older than her 73 years, anything but frail, as if time and experience have toughened rather than weakened her. She sits with her back to the window, through which I could see the waste from the coalmine would have been tipped. I look out at the ruined landscape, but Hettie does not turn to follow my gaze.

I set up, and Hettie peers with suspicion at the digital recorder. 'Is the tape running?'

I explain that there is no tape, but the machine is on and running.

'Shall I start, then? Ok. Well, it was the last day before half-term, see, so I was looking forward to a week off with my cariad Michael. He was going to take me to Barry for a few days – do you know Barry?'

I tell her that I do; I've been there a few times and it's cracking.

'Yeah, a lot of young Saesnegs are going there since that TV programme.'

She positively spits out the S-word, as if it were something unpleasant. I choose not to be surprised by that; instead I register my surprise at her knowledge of BBC sitcoms.

'Anyway,' she says, 'we were all set for half-term at the seaside – yeah, it was off-season and not exactly sunbathing weather, but we liked to get away and it always had to be in the school holidays, what with us both being teachers. Michael taught at Pantglas too, you see. It's how we met.'

I ask if she and Mike had lived together back then.

'That's Michael,' she snaps, 'no one ever called him Mike. And although we were engaged, we never lived together. Unmarried couples didn't back then – especially not in Wales; that would have been a scandal. You should know this, being a history student; don't students do any research these days?'

I feel myself blushing slightly under the pressure of her scolding, and reveal that I am not a history student but study creative writing.

'Oh, that's charming, that is! So you just make it up, then? Well, you're not the only one; Aberfan's been full of that these last fifty years.'

I ask her to elaborate.

'Hundreds of people came to the village, thousands, but not all were here to help. Half of them had only come to get a story for the next day's papers or the evening news. I heard a photographer trying to get a child to cry on demand so he could take the perfect picture. And God help you if you actually spoke to the reporters. We'd never met any before, so we didn't know to be careful – it's a different world to us. They'd turn your words all the wrong way round so you ended up saying exactly what they wanted you to, whether that's what you meant or not. If they'd left us alone, we could have settled down afterwards a lot quicker than we did. I'd like to say it was just the London papers that were making the trouble; but it was some of our own as well, that was what really hurt.'

She looks at me with some hostility. I sense that she doesn't really either understand or welcome my presence, or that of any would-be documentarian, and start to fear that she will end the interview before offering her account. In a bid for her acceptance, I tell her that two of my first cousins Jill and Vincent Parfitt were killed in the disaster. Jill, aged 9, had gone to school as usual that morning while her brother Vincent, aged 13, had needed to go home because he had forgotten his dinner money and was one of the group of four boys that saw the landslide approving the school, two ran one way and survived while Vincent and his friend were killed. I tell her of the way it has affected the family ever since and the sadness I feel at visiting my auntie Joan, now suffering from dementia, asking where Jill and Vincent are and crying because they haven't been to see her.

Hettie reaches out to squeeze my hand as I tell my story, we are sharers of the same deep sadness but when I am finished she resumes her own.

'I still remember the last song playing on the wireless before I left the house: Beach Boys it was, 'Good Vibrations'. I loved that song then but I can't even listen to it now. But it was still in my head when I called at Michael's house. He must have had the wireless on too, because he was whistling it all up the road on the way to school. We passed in the shadow of the waste tips, just like always. They were just part of the landscape by then really; people would say "Oh, those things are going to come down one of these days," but we never thought any more of it.

I got to the school, and there was a real happy atmosphere. All the children were excited about their week off and acting a bit silly. So when this big rumbling noise started up, and got louder and louder, some of them were clapping and cheering in delight. They ran to the window to see it because they thought it was a plane flying over. But planes never flew over here.

Young Rhys, lovely boy he was, said "It's black, Miss, and there's a tree in it!'"

Hettie pauses, dabs at her eyes for a moment, and continues.

'I told the children to get under their desks. I did too, but it came just a few seconds later and the children by the window never made it in time. It hit fast and it hit hard. It blew the windows in first, but that wasn't all. I shouldn't have looked up, but I couldn't help myself. I saw the walls cracking and bending in, and then they were just … gone. And everything went black.'

There follows another long pause. Conscious of the heavy atmosphere, I pause the recorder and offer Hettie a cup of tea.

We drink our tea in silence and I feel guilty for transporting her back to that terrible day.

Hettie drains the last of her tea with a sad sigh.

'My life didn't flash in front of me,' she says. 'When it stopped, there was such an eerie silence. I remember … there was nothing, there was just this numbness. I was trapped up to my waist in desks and rubble and goodness knows what else. I looked up to the roof and I could see a young boy in my class up there, climbing down what was then a tip inside my classroom. The other children were trapped amongst their desks, and I remember this boy climbing down. He climbed to the door; I was trapped nearby, and he started kicking the top half of the door in. So I said to him, "What are you doing?" and he said, "I'm going home". The reality still hadn't registered in me because I felt like giving him a row for breaking the glass. So he kicked the top half of the door in, and then he went out. Suddenly that didn't seem like such a bad idea anymore. When I looked I could see there was enough room for us to crawl through sort of a tunnel. So I went back to the children and I said we had a special fire drill and that if they would crawl through the tunnel then calmly walk across the yard they would be allowed to go straight home. Somebody told me that my quick thinking saved 29 lives that day: I'm not sure that's true, and even if it is, I'll never stop thinking of the children who died in that school.'

There is another long, sad, and difficult silence. I realise with hindsight that I jumped in too early with the break before, and this would have been a better time for tea and sympathy. But Hettie is far from finished, and carries on.

'The five in my class that were killed were just a tiny fraction of the overall death toll. We thought we were the only ones this had happened to, that this monstrosity came hurtling down the hill just for us. But our classroom had only caught a glancing blow from a small offshoot of the main landslide, and other rooms had suffered much worse damage, or been wiped out completely. Like Michael and his class.'

Hettie's hands begin to shake, and she is clearly fighting to try and keep control. She is resolute and manages to refrain from crying, until she notices that I am, and we cry together.

When we resume the interview again, Hettie is composed and frankly, all cried out. She is able to recite the bare facts and statistics with a cold detachment that is, if anything, even more chilling.

'There were 144 deaths in total: 116 children and 28 adults, five of which were teachers at Pantglas. The rescue effort was massive, but basically pointless: by the time the people came flocking in from the other towns, everyone who could be saved had been saved. No one was brought out alive after Jeff Edwards at 11 o'clock.

As soon as the children from my class were moved safely clear, I moved on to the class next door. Was I wrong? I've lost a lot of sleep over that decision this past 50 years; that's for sure. I tell myself that I had done all I could for the children in my classroom, and by moving on I was likely to help someone who had a chance to get out. But that was also Michael's class: was I being selfish? Who was I trying to save: the young man I was supposed to marry, or the two dozen children he had promised to look after, as I had promised to look after mine? This is a question I've asked myself since, but at the time there was nothing in my mind but digging. I was clearing the scree and coal waste as quickly as any of the men; miners with years of pit experience came straight from their shifts to join in the rescue effort, but even they could barely match my pace. They were amazed that this little woman, and I was such a delicate looking thing back then, could work like a miner but it's surprising, you find the strength from somewhere when you have to. It was no use though: that room had taken the full force of landslide head on. We couldn't get any of them out for hours, and by then we knew it would be far too late. No one survived; not Michael, nor any of the children. No one.'

I offer to stop the recording again, but Hettie dismisses the idea with a wave of her hand.

'I've got this far, so I might as well get it over with. The rescue attempts weren't going much better anywhere else. Like I said, reporters arrived by the busload; able bodied men carrying notebooks and cameras instead of picks and shovels. Other well-meaning people came and tried to help, but they just got in the way, scrabbling about with their bare hands and undoing some of the work of the experts. Not that there was anything that could be done by then anyway.

The worst part, by far, came later. A hundred, no a million times worse than actually being under the rubble, was when we had to identify the bodies up at the Bethania chapel. The parents waited in a long line to be let in: I had hoped that they were using it as a hospital, but as I went in, there were people coming out who had been told their children had died. Until then I still had hope that they were waiting for a doctor or had been taken to hospital. When I went, all the pews were covered with little blankets and under them lay the children. My Michael was six foot two though; it took two blankets to cover him, so I spotted him straight away. It was harder for the parents I suppose; some of them had to look under almost every blanket until they finally found their own child.'

I ask, as sensitively as I can, about her husband.

'Well, there were other men, but only Ralph wanted to marry me. Some of them were already married, actually. There was a lot of that went on after the disaster, but they don't report on that so much. Couples couldn't even look at or speak to one another without reminding themselves what had happened, so they'd look to their neighbours for intimacy, or other bereaved parents, or me. I'd close my eyes and imagine they were Michael. It didn't heal my pain, and it didn't heal theirs, but it didn't make it worse either, and that's the best thing you can say about it.

And that was just about all we had to help us get over it anyway. The government didn't help, not really – Labour government it was and all, a Labour Government, a Labour council, and a Labour-nationalised Coal Board, and none of them stood up for us. We had donations from the public, and a disaster fund was set up. But, as you know, we had to use that fund to pay for the removal of the tips – it beggars belief. The Coal Board didn't even have the decency to clear up their own mess; they'd have seen it happen again before putting their hands into their own pockets.'

My final question is to ask what effect the disaster still has today.

'It's fifty years now with the anniversary next month. The rest of Britain will remember us for one day, and then forget again and go back to their lives. But we can never forget. Even those born after it happened, or youngsters whose parents weren't even born then. I've taught successive generations, and they all seem to have something ... missing, and you can't put your finger on what. It's like the whole identity of the village: Aberfan isn't the name of a place anymore; it's the name of a disaster. It looms over the place like those tips once did, just as overbearing and threatening, and it always will, long after everyone who survived that day has been reunited with those who didn't.'

That sounds like a natural point to end so I wrap it up there. I thank Hettie for her time, and on the way out she asks me if I have a title for my work.

'Aberfan,' I say, and she nods. There is nothing more to be said.

HEARTS AND MINDS

A work of fiction, by Pamela Maunsell

'Jack, try and tell me what you're thinking.'

The sound of Laura's voice startled me. I must have drifted off again, thinking about the torti cat. Laura said she was semi-feral, whatever that means. Looking out the French windows, I could see her sitting on the other side of the lawn. Stupid to be so concerned for a cat. I gave myself a mental shakedown and turned back to Laura.

'Sorry, I don't know what's up with me today.'

'Today?'

'I know. I just ... I mean.' I put the brake on my mouth and considered what I really wanted to say. 'I guess you'll be writing your report soon.'

'Does that worry you?

'Not so long as you say I'm fit and ready for duty.' I grinned, 'It's not like I've got PTSD or something. I'm looking forward to getting back to Afghanistan.'

'Are you sure that's what you really want?'

I froze, incredulous. For the first time, I saw Laura as a potential threat. 'Of course, I do.' I was relieved to hear my voice remain strong and steady; no hint of anxiety. She was a therapist, she'd pick up on that sort of thing. Would probably make a meal of it. 'Can't leave the lads out there alone.' I knew I was playing for time. What on earth had given her that notion? I rummaged through my memories of our talks. There was nothing I had said that could have made her think that. What was it then? Maybe, if it wasn't what I'd said, then it was what I hadn't. Bingo.

'Good grief, is this because I haven't talked about Khewa? About what happened there? Sorry, I didn't realise it was compulsory. I usually prefer to focus on the present, that's all.'

She remained silent. I tried not to fidget.

'So, you'll clear me fit, if I tell you about what happened without cracking up?' I said laughing.

'I think, that if you tell me, you'll know if that's what you really want.'

I settled back into the chair, wondering where to begin. After a while I became aware that time was passing and I hadn't opened my mouth. I glanced out of the window again. The cat had crossed the lawn, and was sitting on the patio, watching us like we were part of some soap opera.

It was nothing special, just another 'Hearts and Minds' gig. Five villages in ten days. Our mission: to persuade the locals that we were the good guys, better than the Taliban and, oh so importantly, better than the Yanks. We accomplished this with a mix of listening, gifts and football.

The first four villages had been a doddle. Honestly, so easy. We'd parted with promises to visit again. To return as their honoured guests. One more to go and we'd be back at base.

We arrived in Khewa, after dark. Mahgrib must have just finished and the village was returning to life after prayers. It was only a small place, perhaps 50 white-washed, mud-brick houses; each providing a home for a single family. As protocol demanded, we sought and got permission from the Malik, that's the headman, to set up camp and asked him to convene a meeting of the Jigrha, so that we could meet the rest of the village leaders. Then it was back to camp to discuss strategy and get some food and rest.

'All looks fine to me.' I said. 'What do you think?

Sam grinned. 'Same ol', same ol'.'

Sam was my second-in-command and the only other officer on the trip. He wasn't just a first-class medic, but a linguist and an historian too. The rest of the team were squaddies; mostly on their first tour overseas. Oh, and there was Touma too, our Syrian translator.

'We'll take Touma along, of course.' I said.

'I can translate if you like; give Touma a break.' Sam suggested.

'No.' I was firm about this, 'I need your eyes and ears focused on the meeting, not wondering how much I'm understanding.' A light breeze started up, just enough to set the tent flaps moving and swirl up eddies of sand.

I slept well that night. The silence of the desert that had spooked me so much on my first tour, now familiar and reassuring.

We woke early to an eerily quiet village. That was wrong. Usually, we would be surrounded by a forest of children, all shyly peering at us and bursting into fits of giggles whenever one of us looked at them or spoke. But here there was none.

'Perhaps there's been a death or some illness.' Sam suggested.

'Possible.' But still I felt uneasy. 'Just keep alert.'

'Always,' he snapped back.

I waited to see if he'd go on, say what was bugging him about my command, but when I looked up again he was dusting off his boots.

Around 1100 hours, a young lad came and escorted us to the

Jirga and we spent the next hour doing the listening part of our task. Unlike the other villages, the elders of Khewa had no problems and no grievances. They said they weren't affected by the war, they weren't concerned about supplies and they had access to adequate medical help should it be needed. It was only when I asked if there had been any strangers around, that they looked anxious.

'There is one now.' The Malik said. 'A middle-aged man, travelling with a young boy. He asked to rest for a few days.'

I requested more detailed information, but he simply replied, 'We know no more about them. It is not for us to question our guests.'

I made a mental note to check them out.

We moved on to the gift giving. I like to think our gifts are well chosen. Not like the Americans, who like to laud their wealth. The problem is their presents are just so precious, they can't actually be used. Our gift boxes are always more down-to-earth, things the villagers really need, like chalkboards and chalk, basic medicines, cloth, toiletries and a few sweets for the children. But we always added in one bigger gift and this time it was a pair of solar cookers. Spot on.

The gifts were given and received almost in silence and, shockingly, when we proposed an early evening football match, no one seemed interested.

'I don't like it.' I said, as soon as Sam and I got back to our tent. 'There's something wrong here.'

'But what? You're always getting spooked. It's just some village matter and they want us gone so they can sort it.'

'We'll continue as planned. But if I'm not happy we'll be staying on a while.'

Sam groaned. His wife was due the next day and he was desperate to get back to base.

'One thing though, I definitely want to check out that man and boy. Can't see why the Malik was so reluctant to tell us more. I want to know what their business is in Kandahar.'

As it happens, we didn't have to go looking for them. I was just finishing my second brew when I heard a warning shout from one of the lads. Looking out of the tent flap, I saw a tall, lean man standing absolutely motionless. By his side, a small boy. Both were dressed in the traditional robes of the district.

Sam was already on his feet and out the tent door before I'd had a chance to draw breath. 'Greetings.' He called out in Pashto.

'Asalaam Alaykum. Good Morning to you.' The man responded with a smile before continuing in his native tongue. 'Please forgive this intrusion. I hope I didn't startle your guard. My name is Atif and this,' he said, looking down at the boy, 'is my nephew, Akram.'

The boy stood quietly by his uncle's side, head cast down. Atif was holding Akram's hand, but the boy's body language suggested he wasn't comfortable with that and, I wondered, how hard Atif's grip was.

'How can we help you?' Sam asked.

'It is my nephew for whom I seek a favour.' he answered. 'He so wanted to see your camp and to meet some real Englishmen. Is it possible for him to look around?'

It was hard to believe that the boy had any interest at all. So, what did Atif want? Just curious or was he checking us out?

'His parents died a few weeks ago,' Atif continued, 'and I am taking him to Kandahar. His mother's sister lives there. She will look after him.'

The mention of his parents finally caused the boy to look up at us. There was no mistaking the flash of anger that crossed his face, before his gaze returned to the sand around his feet.

I called for one of the lads to come over. 'You know what to do, hearts and minds, hearts and minds. But keep an eye on the uncle. Let me know if he seems particularly interested in anything.'

'I don't trust him.' I said to Sam.

'Surprise me. Give them a break. He's just a man trying to please a child.' He paused for a while watching the small group. 'Wonder if it was us or the yanks that did for his parents?'

The next morning, I got the lads assembling the solar cooker. It only takes about 30 minutes and once it was ready, they'd do a demo for the village women (accompanied by their menfolk of course). This was the other thing I loved about the cookers; the delight on the women's faces and the 'what about us' look on the men's as they realised the main gift wasn't for them.

'What do you think, Sam? Do we leave tomorrow?'

'For sure. Nothing has happened to warrant us staying. Ok, I admit the village hasn't been that welcoming, but heck, that's not a capital offence.'

'I'm not sure. Somethings adrift, I just can't place it. I don't like that Atif; I suspect it's his presence that's at the root of all this.'

'All what? You're jumping at shadows.' Sam was getting cranky with my suspicions. 'Get some sleep, tomorrow we'll be back at base.'

Reluctantly I made the decision to leave. I'd file reports back at base and someone would monitor Atif's arrival in Kandahar.

The next morning, we rose early and the lads loaded the lorries and cleaned the area, leaving it as spotless as we found it. I was just about to give the order to leave when we heard a shout. Atif was running towards us, his robes half hitched up.

'Again, I have come to ask you for your help', he said. 'I understand that you are going to Kandahar and I am wondering if it I might impose upon you and ask that Akram accompany you?' He paused to draw breath. 'His little feet are blistered and it is a long walk for such a small chap.'

I looked at Sam, who nodded in agreement. 'Okay, but he has to be here in five minutes.' I could feel the tension inside me but what could be wrong?

'Why didn't he come with you?'

'He was worried you'd say no. He'd be so embarrassed.'

We watched Atif jog back across the sand.

'Here he comes,' Sam yelled over the sound of revving engines. 'Let's put him in Touma's car. There'll be space enough there.'

Akram wasn't rushing. Shoulders bent, he plodded towards us. Where was Atif? Surely, he'd come to see the lad off? He looked so vulnerable and so down-hearted. Not even a flicker of excitement at riding in a Land Rover, probably the first car he'd ever been in. I tried to reassure myself, he'd just lost his family, he was losing his uncle and going to live with a family he didn't know and he had a day's ride ahead with total strangers. With every step he took, my unease grew, until it was crashing around me, something begging to be noticed, setting my heart thumping and my palms sweating. Akram walked like a condemned man. Then I looked again, it was his posture, it was all wrong, I tried to work out a reason. Blistered feet? Tiredness? Anxiety? And then I got it.

I grabbed Sam. 'Order him to stop.'

Sam knew to obey a direct order, even one he couldn't

comprehend. He yelled out, 'Stop! Stay where you are.'

But the little boy just kept trudging on.

'Tell him to stop or I'll shoot.'

Sam glanced at me in horror, but gave the order. It had no effect. Akram walked on. He must have sensed me raising my gun, as it was then that he lifted his head and looked me straight in the eyes; and we both knew the truth and we both knew each other knew it too.

'Stop! Stop! Stop!' Sam was beside himself, shouting in both Pashto and English. Pleading with the boy, begging him to obey.

I fired a single warning shot, but he didn't break stride. Instead he looked at me as if begging me to bring it all to an end.

I did. I fired. A single shot to the head.

Normal protocol demands a body shot, because a body presents a larger target, but you can't go for a body shot when someone's wearing a bomb belt.

'It's alright Jack, you're safe now, you're safe.' Laura's voice cut through the sound of my screams.

'Oh, God. I'm sorry.' I said. 'That must have been horrible to watch.'

'You've been "gone" a good while.'

But I was still too disorientated to respond. I tried to get my bearings and bring my heart rate down. I needed to get some air. I opened the French doors and the cool breeze was soothing. From down below me there was a tentative 'meow'. The cat was sitting in a flower pot, soaking up the sun which flooded the garden. When she realised she had my attention she turned her head to start washing her flank. It took me a couple of minutes to steady myself before I was able to return to my chair.

'You were right. I don't want to go back. I can't possibly go back, do that again.'

'I know.'

I could feel my breathing ease. 'I thought I'd feel different, cowardly, disloyal. It's like I've crossed some sort of divide. I don't think I could do the job even if I wanted to.'

The silence, that followed, felt comfortable.

We said our goodbyes. I thanked her for her time and for her patience. I would never know how much of my story she'd heard or how much had been scrambled in my panic attack. But I did know it didn't matter.

Just before I left, I took a last look out of the window, wanting to bid farewell to the cat but she had already turned away and was walking off across the lawn.

FOUR STAGES OF LOVE

A work of fiction, by Ayse Morris

I gazed out of the window as I often did these days, the same old same view, only the season had changed again. The wind caused the curtains to flutter silently and gracefully. The cool breeze that swept my face carried the sound of the children's laughter from the school across the road into the room. My chest tingled as my memory saw Michael in the playground playing football, if only he could do that now instead of lying in the bed all day. I visualised his gappy grin, pale blue eyes and freckles; he certainly stood out. The trousers he wore were too short, his mouth was too big.

Strawberry blonde hair – that complemented his eyes – stuck up at the front, much to my annoyance. The urge to lick my hand and pat his quiff down, as my mother did to my brother, was tempting.

How my blood had boiled over his classroom antics back then, his showing off wasted as my back was turned on him more than once, in fact, it was the one thing I did the most each day. As much as he tried to get my attention with his loudness and silly voices, I was having none of it! He took pleasure in sitting at the desk in front of me, tipping his chair back on two legs and banging himself on my desk, thud, thud, thud. My head was bent down as I tried to write, my hand rigid on my pencil so much so that I was sure it would snap clean in two. How I wished that he would disappear. He was not getting a reaction!

Now and then I would steal a glance, just to see what

shenanigans he was up to. Every time that I was caught, he would wink cheekily. I felt hot and tearful, chastising myself for getting caught out. I looked away in disgust, he was vile! My friend Margaret heard this frequently as we played two balls up the wall.

One such day by the hopscotch, Margaret was quite dramatic trying to pick up her slate. As she wobbled on one leg, her drawers were showing to all and sundry. Not being the best view on offer that day, my head turned to look around. I saw him in the distance playing bulldog, I watched a while as he led the game as he always did. He flashed a smile, my cheeks burned and my stomach fluttered. Who does he think he is? Turning my head abruptly back to Margaret – who I was thankful had now managed to cover her undergarments, I made a huge decision that I would NOT look at that boy again.

On Monday morning we sat in assembly, back straight with legs crossed.

'All things bright and beautiful, the Lord God made them all' we sang in unison.

I glanced over, and for my troubles, he blew me a kiss! Ugh! How uncouth! Silly boy! Revolted, I turned to face the red-faced headmaster leading assembly as he sung his heart out. Every now and then trying to side-glance at Michael, but he was sitting a little behind, it was impossible! Each time reminding myself I should not be looking.

One evening as we played out on unlit streets, as the sun was setting, Michael was dared to make a move.

'Kiss her, go on, do it,' his friends chanted.

'Here, Jennifer, want a kiss?' he offered.

'No!!' I could feel my face burning.

I stood my guard, rolled my eyes and wished this joker away. Turning my head I linked Margaret's arm and we stomped off down the street to go home. Every now and then I would glance over my shoulder, inside my chest my heart fluttered. I wished the night away as I did every night to see him again in the morning, but I wasn't going to let him know that!

He stood out with his cheeky grin, slicked combed red-tinged hair, yet it was his sparkling blue eyes that really caught my stare. His gappy teeth gone, replaced by perfectly polished pearls, yet the cheekiness in his wide smile was evident still, even after all these years. Walking towards him with my head bowed, my mouth was so dry my lips were sticking to my teeth. My hands were shaking and sweating in my dress gloves, the drum in my chest banged its own beat. There was a confusion of knots and butterflies entwining each other in my tummy. Much the same as when we were kids but more intense.

He was smart in his sharp-cut suit with crimson tie, gone was the scruffy kid of old. Not a hair out of place, a perfect quiff sitting centre. He looked petrified! Ever the joker, now in this moment he appeared so serious, his extroversion withdrawing. His eyes spoke all the words that were needed, drawing me in I felt his emotion and was reassured instantly when he took my hand. My heart all but bursts with pride as my excitement rises like lemonade bubbles racing to the top of the glass. He is beautiful, a work of art, chiselled, defined and expressive. He is radiant.

'Hello, Michael'

'Hello, Jenny, you look beautiful, shall we go?

He took my hand and squeezed it as we strode in silence. My heart had gone from casual canter to full-blown gallop. I imagined his arms around me, holding me close, tight and protective, carrying me on a wave of contentment.

The ballroom was classy. Chandeliers surrounded by nineteenth-century plaster roses hung from the high ceilings, shimmering their light around the ballroom. Red velvet seats with dark polished wooden tables awaited tired dancers and sore feet. The polished floor shone with the lights' reflection illuminating the couples moving across the floor. A live band were playing dressed in tuxedos, it looked well-to-do in there. Our heels echoed as we stepped across the floor to find our seats.

Michael took my coat off and hung it neatly over the chair. The band started to play Glenn Miller's 'In the mood'. Michael looked at me and stretched out his arm, I took his hand and we made our way to the dance floor. I hadn't been dancing before, in my bedroom practising with Margaret, who was as gangly as she was clumsy, had not helped me prepare for this moment. My dress swished one way, overlapping as it swished back again as we jived on the dance floor. Michael's hair flopped to the side as he moved, beads of sweat balanced on his brow, falling with sudden movement. He loosened his tie to cool down. We had danced so much, the band were brilliant.

We sat and drank cola out of glass bottles and stripy straws. Michael told me about the job he had obtained in the postal room at a posh office block in London and how he was going to work his way up. We hadn't seen each other around that often once we went to secondary school. Michael had lost his mum and had gone to live with his nan due to his dad working a lot. It was by chance when he was visiting his dad that we bumped into each other.

The night was over too quickly, my feet were tired yet I breathed a heavy sigh and smiled, all good things had to come to an end. The cool air hit us as we walked out into the evening. It was welcomed. We strode along the promenade, the illuminations attracting the crowd of people busy going home after their evenings out or like us making it last a little longer. We ate fish and chips under the bright lights, looking out over the blackness of the beach. The moon's reflection swaying with the movement of the sea was soothing and tranquil, there was no other place I would want to be. Michael walked me home. He told me I was a great dancer, I was equally complimentary. We stood by my front gate as Michael spoke.

'Thank you for a lovely evening'.

'The pleasure was all mine'.

'Never thought I would hear you say I was a pleasure'.

We laughed. I looked up at him. He searched my eyes as his darted from side to side, with a nervous half-laugh he leant in and kissed me on the lips. His lips wet, cold and soft. Inside my body exploded like fireworks going off in every direction, touching every crevice.

I was complete and safe, I would be for the rest of my life. I trusted him, loved him, even though it was unclear how this happened, I was sure I always had.

I watched him pat down Jason's hair.

'Ugh, Dad, don't wet your hand'

I smiled at the memories that came to me, how had we gone

from primary school revulsion, to teenage dating and marriage so quickly. Tingling with happiness I looked on as he tumbled to the floor and our children scrambled on his back to play horsey.

'Giddy up horsey,' they chanted.

Michael did the circuit of our living room, crawling around on our floral, hessian backed carpet. His knees sore by the time they got off of his back. He stood up holding the mantelpiece and rubbed his back and knees. Cherishing these moments every single day showed me how lucky we are to have him. I admired him as a father, especially moments like when he cheated at Scrabble.

'Of course, it is a word!' he would say convincingly.

Except the children were not convinced at all, we watched as he opened the dictionary pretending to look for the word that did not exist. Our children leaning in, looking on quietly in anticipation. Eyes following every page turn waiting for him to say something. Then he'd shut the book so hard it slammed with a big bang! Our children jumped ten feet in the air.

'See, I told you all!'

I watched my children laugh hard. Twinkling eyes and scrunched up noses.

'There is NO such word,' they shouted between laughter.

'Of course, there is! You weren't quick enough to see it'.

The children turned each page of the dictionary to find the word that deep down they knew did not exist, but they looked regardless in case it was true. That night as the children slept contented, I stood in the doorway of the living room leaning on the frame, head resting to one side, tea towel over my arm from drying the dishes and stared at him. His feet were on the pouffe, his socks hanging off the end of his toes. His head had fallen to the side and he was breathing heavily, not quite a snore but a contented slumber.

Michael's day was busy, it always was. Rising at 06:00, out by 07:00 to catch the train to London, home at 18:30. Dinner was barely consumed and the children were taking full advantage of his time. He was exhausted every evening but he didn't care for himself, he only cared about us and our happiness. There was no asking for time to read his paper, a bath or a cup of tea. The children wanted to play and play he would.

He opened his eyes and saw me. After a stretch, he rose to his feet, took the tea towel from my arm and informed me he would finish up. Little prickles of pain stabbed at my heart, one day I thought, when the children are older, I will find a job and help ease his day.

I closed the curtains a little. The breeze had got stronger and flowed through the room. I have to avoid him catching a chill as the illness weakens his immune system. Opening a magazine I flicked through. Recipes for the perfect dinner party with little prep time, an agony aunt page. I am curious to what her advice to me would be. Turning the page I find a large crossword. Pulling out my pen I attempted to waste some time as Michael sleeps most of the day.

We had liked to do crosswords together, Michael had a knack for them. Often I would get excited by my answer and then the word would not fit in the letter spaces; he would laugh at me. There is no solid answer this time.

His movement is still. He rarely moves, unless he is turned to prevent bed sores. There is no interest in getting up and joining the other residents. To speak takes effort, he gets muddled and stutters, which frustrates him. Then, another day, it is like this never happened. He would be sitting up reading the paper and chatting away. One time he asked Kathy the cook out. She joked she would love to but his wife might have something to say, she gestured to me. He looked over at me.

'She can come too I suppose'.

It was funny to everyone except me, inside it gnawed at my stomach. The realisation that my husband doesn't know who I am on most days. Acceptance is hard.

His hair no longer sticks up, he can no longer comb it to the side and build up his perfect Elvis Presley quiff. He doesn't have much now and what he has is grey and thinning. The muscles in his legs are weak. They exercise his legs daily to help his muscle tone, but not quite to the standard where he used to work, garden or play football, no those days are forever gone.

The jokes are redundant except for the odd occasion he returns to me, these are rare and precious occasions that I grasp with all my might. There are no personal jokes between us any more, where we would playfully mock one another. My chest feels like it is about to cave in, burning bile creeps up to my throat as it hits me again that our marriage as we knew it is gone.

Michael stirs asking for a drink. I place the straw to his mouth and he sips it slowly. The illness, not content with taking his memory, is restricting his swallowing action. I wipe the residue with a tissue.

He looks at me, I look back at him and smile. It is obvious that he does not want me to see him like this, the hurt is evident in his eyes. Within minutes it is likely to fade and he could go back to the bubble that surrounds him, and he'll wonder who I am. The bubble where he is oblivious to the world around him, or the confusion will surface like last Christmas. I had put a small tree in his room, he asked me what toys I had bought the children.

Looking at each other speech is not needed, not really, his love is felt on the occasions he comes back to me. It is as if I can see through his eyes in to his soul and feel his emotion. The power of our love is evident when he squeezes my hand, like on the first date at the ballroom where on the crest of a wave of nerves, excitement and happiness ran through me. Momentarily I am back in his arms wrapped tight around me as I sink into them.

This is the end of our love story as we knew it. He is looking at me intensely, and I see him. Those pale blue eyes with the little Irish sparkle, that stupid gappy grin – my Michael. He is there, deep and far away maybe, but he is there all the same. At times I am treated to a wink, a hint that on that day he knows. He knows I am his Jenny, and he is back in the playground where he fell in love with me.

NEW BEGINNINGS

A work of fiction, by Karen Simmonds

My Darling Nick,

You'd absolutely adore this place. There's the workshop you always wanted, the vegetable patch for me and beautiful fragrant floribunda roses framing the wooden front door. Of course, it needs decorating and some tlc but it is the home we dreamed of. Paxton loves it and it's all I can do to get him in at night, he's too interested in the smells in every corner of the garden. I've picked all the runner beans and given some to Claire and Mike and I'm using the other vegetables for chutneys. There's way too much for me! Claire and I are having a girl's day tomorrow looking at paint and wallpaper; I need to put our stamp on it. I wish you were picking the colours with me.

I miss you more every day, love always.

Jane

A deep-throated chuckle echoed round the staffroom. Her entrance stopped the room dead as all heads turned in her direction. To her relief, a big warm hand cupped her elbow guiding her to the coffee machine,

'You'll be needing one of these. They're not so bad, just not used to new members of staff . I'm Eleanor James, Deputy Head. You must be Mrs Morgan.'

'Yes, Jane Morgan. Newbie!' She twiddled with her wedding and engagement rings.

'Don't worry, the children won't bite!' She smiled, handing her the steaming hot cup. 'Nervous?'

'Thanks. Yes, it's been a while. I'll be ok after the first day.' She twiddled with her wedding and engagement rings again. She sighed and thought of Nick's first day at work at St.Margaret's Primary School, tears forming in her azure blue eyes. She gently gripped the handle as she drained her coffee. 'Is there anything I should know before I meet the children?'

'A very nice group of children, a couple of spirited ones but nothing to worry about.'

As she finished, the sound of the bell wailed round the staffroom and all the teachers sprang into action, grabbing their books and bags. The room cleared in less than two minutes. Jane relaxed as she felt the familiar hand on her elbow.

'I'll take you to your room and introduce your Teaching Assistant, Miss Jones.'

Eleanor grabbed her books and guided Jane through the throng in the corridor. Like little ants, bodies were marching towards their classrooms. Jane couldn't help but smile. They came to a halt and opened a door to the left. As she entered she passed a neat row of name-tagged coats and boots tied together with pegs and entered the hullabaloo of the Year 3 classroom. She was hit by a myriad of colours, words and giggles. Sets of eyes peered at her as she made her way to her desk at the front of the classroom. Mrs James introduced her,

'Children, this is Mrs Morgan. She'll be your new teacher for this year. Let's welcome her to St.Mary's.' The pitter patter of tiny hands was only just audible over the thumping of her heart. Jane smiled.

'Good morning, children. I hope to speak to all of you today and learn everyone's name. If you have any questions please come to the front and see me.' Her confidence grew as their eyes softened. She took a deep breath and sat at her desk.

'Mrs Morgan, this is Kate. She has something for you.' Miss Jones let go of a small hand and a little figure appeared from behind her, 'She's very shy' she mouthed.

'Hello Kate, it's nice to meet you. What did you want to show me?' As the small figure walked round the desk, a tiny hand proffered a colourful picture. 'That's very good, is it for me?'

A little voice whispered, 'Yes, Mrs Morgan. You looked a bit sad.'

'Thank you Kate, that's very kind. Do you like drawing?' she asked gently.

'Yes, Mrs Morgan. I draw for my Daddy.'

'I bet he likes those. What about your Mummy, does she like them?' A sad look crossed Kate's face before the words came out of her tiny mouth.

'My Mummy went to heaven' she whispered as she looked down at her shiny black shoes.

'I'm sorry, Kate. Why don't you draw your Daddy one now, I'm sure he'd like that.' She scooped up the little hand in hers and led her back to her seat. One look at the hidden sadness in the little girls face melted her heart.

Miss Jones smiled as she approached, 'Did anyone mention Kate's situation to you?'

'No, nobody. How long ago?'

'About eight months ago. Breast cancer. She's coping ok but understandably gets upset at times.' They turned to watch Kate as she focused on her drawing.

'She's a gifted artist, even at that age. Is that how she copes?' Jane wondered aloud.

'Yes,' replied Miss Jones. 'Her Mum was a potter so she's been around art and artists. She seems happy when she's drawing.' She turned back to face Jane, 'I'm sorry no one told you.'

'Is there anything else I can do?' Jane asked.

'Just be yourself, she seems to like you,' said Miss Jones as she wandered over to tidy the books on the bookshelf.

'Just checking in. So how was your first day?' Claire, straight to the point as usual. Even down the telephone Jane could picture her holding a glass of Pinot Grigio, sitting on the edge of her snuggle chair.

'6 o'clock on the dot, it could only be you,' chuckled Jane. 'It was strange going back into a classroom after so long but was really nice. They're a lovely bunch of children. I just miss Nick being here so I can tell him about my day.' She sank back in her chair and wrapped herself in her favourite blanket. Paxton jumped up on her lap as if he knew.

'The first day was always going to be the hardest. Tomorrow will be better. You know I'm here if you need me, any time. We'll catch up for lunch soon.'

'Looking forward to it. Thanks for everything. Hugs.'

As Jane put the phone down, she suddenly got the desire for a nice cold glass of Pinot. Claire's influence had rubbed off on her over the past year. With a glass in one hand and a magazine in the other, she lounged on the sofa and thought about Kate.

My Darling Nick

The house is coming on a treat. Claire helped me paint the front room and the kitchen. I love the big Aga though it has taken some getting used to. I still make your favourite cake every Sunday, except now I take the leftovers into work on Monday.

We're off to the zoo this week. Do you remember when we went to the zoo with our picnic? Even eating in the car, sheltering from the rain was fun. A day we'll never forget! Kate still draws me pictures every week and I now have quite a collection on the fridge. They are always bright, colourful pictures. She is like the daughter we always wanted. Claire has told me she is expecting a baby in May. I'm really happy for her but tinged with sadness for us. They'll make great parents.

I miss you more every day, love always.

Jane

The dappled sunshine blinded Jane as she drew the curtains. Paxton knew what that meant as he tumbled down the stairs and sat, waiting patiently, at the back door. Jane stumbled down the stairs yawning, narrowly missing Paxton's well-gnawed bone.

'Paxton, you really should be careful where you leave your bones!'

She smiled as she rubbed behind his ears, his big brown eyes filled with excitement and his tail wagging non-stop. Neither one bored of the shared affection.

'Ok, go get them!' said Jane excitedly. Paxton barged his way through the backdoor in a hurry to find the plump pigeons that regularly teased him from the fencepost. He'd soon lose interest and instead start sniffing the garden for the scent of any nocturnal intruders. He was careful to avoid Jane's vegetable patch and the bed of roses.

As the kettle boiled to a whistling crescendo, Jane heard letters drop on the mat. Paxton heard it too and made a bee-line straight for the junk mail. It saves me a job she thought as he shredded his way through replacement window and fast food offers. Grabbing her steaming coffee and, with a croissant stuffed crookedly in her mouth, sank into the bean bag chair in the sun-dappled conservatory. Paxton sat at her feet, ready to catch any falling crumbs of croissant. As she finished her coffee, Paxton was suddenly standing at the front door, lead in mouth. They both bundled through the door into the fresh air, Jane tripped over a winter pansy that had been carefully placed on the step. A beautiful buttery colour peeking out from behind a jungle of green leaves. She looked around but the plant bearer had disappeared. She frowned as she opened the rickety gate and trotted down the lane behind Paxton.

Halfway round her usual route, Jane was feeling the burn, mentally and physically. The warmth of the sun was enough for her to strip to her vest. Paxton was at her side keeping up with every step. Her mind had been so preoccupied with the plant that she hardly noticed the fallen leaves crunching and the familiar birdsong that blended with them. She loved village life and the freedom it offered both her and Paxton. She could never have enjoyed her Saturday mornings in East London with the pollution, heavy traffic and anti-social behaviour on every corner. And now there was a mystery person leaving her presents. She'd plant it later when she was digging over her vegetable patch. Village life had lots of surprises.

My Darling Nick,

Winter is just about here and I've prepared the garden ready for next spring. It's going to look so pretty with daffodils, crocuses and tulips lining the path. I have invited your parents and my Mum for Christmas; hope I can use the Aga by then! The last month has flown by. It's quite strange as winter pansies keep appearing on my doorstep. I have planted most of them in front of the roses but I'll have to keep the rest outside in their pots as the ground's too hard to plant anything. I've got involved in the St Mary's children's choir and practice with them once a week. They're all so excited about the Christmas concert, I am too. Claire and Mike have just got back from Grand Cayman Island so I haven't seen her much. I'm looking forward to getting together with them, though it won't be the usual drunken shenanigans for Claire.

I miss you more every day, love always.

Jane

A little hand tugged at her sleeve, 'Mrs Morgan, this is my Daddy.'

'Hi, I'm Sam' came a voice with an accent she couldn't place. He extended his warm hand and Jane shook it. 'The concert was marvellous, the choir were in fine voice. It's all Kate's been talking about for the last few weeks.'

'I'm really glad. Kate has been very enthusiastic and seems to have enjoyed it. Maybe she has a promising future in the arts as she has a wonderful voice.'

'Her Mum's genetics I'm afraid, I'm not that creative.' He put his arm protectively round Kate's shoulders.

'You should be proud, she is very talented.' She smiled as Kate giggled.

'Daddy, I'm going to see Charlotte. I'll come back when I've talked to her.' With that Kate skipped off to find her friend.

'Would you like a drink? I was just off to get one myself after all the excitement' grinned Jane.

'Why not' sighed Sam, 'I don't think we'll be going anywhere any time soon!'

Jane passed Sam a glass of wine as she waved to parents ushering their weary children home as it was getting late in the evening. His face told Jane something was troubling him. 'I'm glad I have the chance for a quick word. It's about Kate. I'm not really sure how to put it,' he shuffled, looked at the wine then took a big mouthful. 'Since you joined the school, she's been talking about you non-stop.'

Jane blushed and took a mouthful of her wine.

'She wanted to cheer you up as she thought you looked sad. That's why she's been leaving winter pansies in your garden. We walk past every week and she asked if she could leave plants for you. She didn't want you to know who they were from.' It was Sam's turn to blush. 'I hope you don't mind.'

She smiled, 'Not at all. Their appearance has baffled me. It's really sweet of her.' Her shoulders relaxed as she started to piece things together.

Sam continued, 'Since Alice, her Mum, passed away she hasn't really had any female influences in her life. I only have a brother and my Mum passed away some time ago. For some reason Kate has really taken to you and feels comfortable with you. She is a caring child and is always thinking of other people, despite what she's been through.' He fidgeted as tears started to well in his eyes. Jane instinctively touched his arm.

'I'm glad she feels she can talk to me and is comfortable around me. I can't imagine what she, and you, has been through. It's a cliché but these things take time. Believe me; I know what it's like to lose someone you love. I went through that a year ago. Ever since then, I write my husband letters telling him what's going on in my life. It's hard no matter how old you are. On the outside people think you're coping really well but inside ...' It was her turn to start welling up. 'Look at us both, on such a happy evening. We can't let the children see us like this.' She finished her wine as Kate came skipping back to collect her dad.

'Daddy, we need to go home soon as Oscar needs feeding,' she

STORIES FROM EVERYWHERE – AN ANTHOLOGY

said insistently.

'The dog,' whispered Sam.

'I have to go home and see to Paxton as well, my dog' replied Jane.

'Oh Daddy, can we walk Oscar with Paxton? We could do it this Saturday, and then have lunch,' excitement creeping into her voice.

'Maybe Mrs Morgan already has plans as it's nearly Christmas.' He turned to Jane, 'On the off chance, and at short notice, are you free on Saturday afternoon as I believe my daughter would like us to walk our dogs and have lunch!'

Kate stood between them looking at one then the other. 'Please Mrs Morgan.'

She smiled, 'As it happens I am free. I will ask Paxton if he'd like to meet Oscar. I'm sure he'll say yes. What time?'

Sam picked Kate up in his arms, 'Shall we say about 10? How about we come and knock as we pass, and go from there.'

'That sounds perfect. Kate, I'll see you in class tomorrow. Sam, I'll see you with Oscar on Saturday morning.' She smiled and gently patted Kate's back. With that, Sam turned and followed the last few parents and performers through the door. Jane turned and smiled to herself.

My Darling Nick

Christmas was nice, but wasn't quite the same. I'm glad your parents made it, and yes the Aga was fine! I'm still enjoying St. Mary's and am getting the choir ready for the Easter concert after the success of the Christmas one. I have been out with Kate, her dad and the dogs a few times and enjoy their company. We seem to be going through the same stage in life. We have provisional plans for half term. Kate is slowly coming out of her shell and turning into quite the young lady. Life in the village is as nice as I'd hoped.

I still miss you terribly but have made some good friends and have thrown myself into the local community as a distraction. I'm doing ok and feel positive about the future for the first time in 18 months.

I miss you more every day, love always.

Jane

THE GIRL IN BLUE

The opening section of a novel, by Emma-Marie Smith

There's a car, its red-streaked windows dappled with rain. Long white fingers curl around a steering wheel. I look up and see dark eyes pocketed in pallid skin, a purple mouth pulled taught. The man's face is vivid to me now, but by the time I wake it will have faded, the image receded into some dark corner of my brain, never to be seen again.

The car swallows yellow road markings. It's picking up pace, the leather seats juddering as it veers down a steep, grassy bank towards a stretch of green canal. The windscreen wipers are frantic as the wheels thud over mounds of grass.

The car lurches downhill and I know it's too late.

'Stop,' I say. 'Please stop.' But the man's eyes are fixed ahead as if I'm not there. I try the door, it's locked. I try the windows, they're locked too. When I swing my head back to the driver's seat, the man is gone.

The car skids towards the dark expanse of water, crashing through a fence at the bottom of the bank. I grab the wheel, feeling around with my foot for the brake pedal, but it's hopeless. I can't drive. It's too late.

I'm going to die. I know that now. I let the fear claw at my chest, then dissipate. The river swallows me whole. It will be a relief, I think. Death will come as a relief. There's nothing to do now. Nothing to do but close my eyes and wait for the darkness.

The darkness comes quickly, settling over me like dust. Silence hums in my ears. There's a musty smell, like wet washing. I'm shivering, teeth chattering, and my legs and feet are bare. I curl my toes into the ground, my unpainted nails scratching at cold stone.

Am I outside? I can't be, I can hear the low hum of electricity, of life, and there's no sky overhead. There is a ceiling, and a small square of light cutting through the darkness. A window? No, a hatch door. There's something else in the corner, something big, mechanical. If I squint, I can trace its outline. It's partly lit by the slices of light from the hatch. It looks like some kind of lift, though I can't think what it could be used for. There's a switch on the wall, a gem of red light, and an iron lever with a handle. Everything else is blanketed in darkness.

I claw at my memories, trying to work out where I am, but there's nothing concrete, nothing definite. Only speculation. A basement, perhaps. Or a cellar. Buried alive. No, not that. Focus on the square of light, try not to panic.

I strain my eyes against the darkness. There are no windows, no doors, just the light from the hatch. The ceiling is low, too low for me to stand up straight. I'm not sure my legs will work anyway, but I have to try. I reach a hand into the darkness and grope around. Nothing. I feel around behind my back. There's a wall, more stone. I am propped against it, but not tied up, not bound. I can move freely, that's good. I take a breath and struggle to my feet.

Pain buckles my knees, slices through my core. I slide back down the wall and onto the cold stone, unable to think clearly until it subsides. I touch the area between my legs carefully, trying not to shake. I'm wearing pants made out of paper. There's a thick wodge of something inside, like a large sanitary towel. Everything is wet with blood. Breathe. Try not to panic. Try not to think the worst.

I'm still for a moment, my fingers numb with cold, trying to remember. I have to try again. I have to get out. But my head spins and I think of the blood. Maybe I should wait. Wait for what? Wait

STORIES FROM EVERYWHERE – AN ANTHOLOGY

to be killed, or worse? Will anyone be looking for me? Claire, maybe, though we sometimes go weeks without talking on the phone. What about Amber and Geoffrey Madison? They wouldn't necessarily think anything was wrong, even if I've missed work. I've come in late before, after a heavy night. I imagine police hammering on doors, sniffer dogs on leads. But it could have only been a few hours since I was last seen. It could have been days. I try to remember the last person I saw, but the fog descends again, and no matter how badly I try to grasp the memory, it curls in the air like smoke and disappears.

Maybe this is just like waking in the night, disorientated, and having to turn a light, wait for reality to come flooding back. That happens to me sometimes. Sit up, open the curtains, reach for my phone. Breathe in the night air. Listen to the sirens on the streets, the endless rumble of engines in the night. There will be an explanation. But I wait and wait and nothing happens. No comforting light, no hand on my back telling me it's all a dream. Only silence. Silence in my head, silence all around.

I explore my body for clues. I can't see bruises but I can feel them. My limbs are heavy, sore, as if I've been in an accident. Maybe I have. Would that explain the car in my dream? I remember it more vividly than I remember anything from my own life. Panic bubbles in my stomach. My breasts prickle under an itchy top. As I go to scratch the skin, I realise I'm not wearing a bra. I reach my arms up and feel two squares of Velcro secured at the nape of my neck like the fastening of a hospital gown. Could it be?

There's a hooded sweatshirt around my shoulders, unzipped. It's my favourite, the navy blue one with the chewed white toggles. Memories dredge up through the darkness. Being huddled in that hoodie in front of my laptop at university, the fuzz of another hangover thick in my head; lying crumpled in Mum's arms after a break-up, the sleeves sodden with tears and snot; coming home to my empty flat after her funeral, stripping off my dress and tights and pulling it on before crawling into bed. I can't see it, but I can feel the soft cotton around me, the cuffs stiff from too many washes.

There's something else too, something tight around my wrist. I think it's a hospital band. I strain my eyes as I twist it around, looking for information, but it's hopeless. My sight is bad enough in broad daylight without my glasses. I wear glasses. Good, I can remember that. Anything else? My name. That's a good place to start – everyone has a name. Bethany Ainshaw, Beth for short. That part's easy. Age? Twenty-six. Easy again. 'Beth Ainshaw. Twenty-six.' I mutter the words to myself, worried that if I let them go, they'll slip out of reach.

I can't just sit here, no concept of time, no idea where I am. I'm terrified I'll make the bleeding worse, or pass out on the cold stone and knock myself unconscious. But I'm more scared to do nothing, to just slowly fade away.

The square of light in the ceiling has dulled. I have to move now before it gets dark. I haul myself to my feet and grip the wall for support. I can just about stand if I duck my head slightly, but my legs are unsteady. I don't know how long I'll last on my feet. I feel my way along the wall in the direction of the hatch, the tiny fragments of light fading from view. I can't let the darkness come, can't let it overpower me. I have to get to the hatch. I tread slowly along the wall, my legs trembling, until my hand grips on to something. A slim glass cylinder connected to a pipe trails down the wall. I feel around. There are other identical cylinders lined up in rows. More pipes slither down the stone.

I stub my toe on something.

'Shit.' The word echoes between the walls and makes me jump.

I can't see anything but the lift, far away from me at the end of this room. I crouch down, feeling around in front of me, and touch metal. Smooth, round metal. I trace the shapes with my fingers. Beer barrels stacked on top of one another, their bodies cold. There are others, too, raised by racks like cattle, their faces tipped forwards. I follow one of them right down to its mouth, to a long plastic tap with a turnkey. I twist it between my fingers and lukewarm liquid gushes over my hands, splashing my feet and legs. A distinctive smell hits the back of my throat. Beer, I think, more specifically draught beer. The ones attached to the glass cylinders are lagers, flushed through chilling pipes. I don't know how I know that.

One of the cylinders splutters to life and there's a sound like liquid filling a glass. The pipe hisses. I hear footsteps overhead, then the murmur of a low voice, as if someone is humming or singing.

'Help.' I hammer on the ceiling above. 'I'm down here. Help me. Please.'

Nothing happens. I strain my ears, but I can no longer hear the footsteps or the muffled voice.

'Please. Is anyone there?'

My heart thuds in my chest. Did I imagine those noises? Am I going mad already? The square of light is grey now, and I can't get to it unless I climb over the stacks of barrels. Before long, I won't be able to see anything at all. Just blankness. Darkness – and for how long?

More footsteps back and forth, coming closer, then retreating. A door opens somewhere upstairs. I clutch on to one of the pipes for support. The footsteps are close now. Shoes tap and click the floorboards. A slow, purposeful stride. They stop, just above me. The room is flooded with flickering yellow light.

FOUR POEMS

Poetry, by Rosie Toye

1. Hours of Darkness

We wonder what goes on at night –
a mother wakes when baby cries,
strange things occur when out of sight.

Someone struggles through their last fight,
an old man sleeps as his wife dies.
We wonder what goes on at night –

feeling alone, although held tight,
a wife is duped by husband's lies,
strange things occur when out of sight.

Doomed affairs cause much sad plight,
parting lovers say sad good-byes.
We wonder what goes on at night –

creatures crawl and fierce vampires bite,
children scream and cover their eyes,
strange things occur when out of sight.

Figures appear all robed in white,
ghosts and angels roam darkened skies.
We wonder what goes on at night –
strange things occur when out of sight.

2. Another Missed Opportunity

But for her, it could have been me.
At the venue, I saw him first,
I looked his way; he didn't see.
This always happens, I am cursed.

At the venue, I saw him first,
she sidled past with charm and poise.
This always happens, I am cursed.
I am no-one. I have no voice.

She sidled past with charm and poise,
she blocked my presence, cut my line.
I am no-one. I have no voice.
My chance gone – he could have been mine.

She blocked my presence, cut my line,
determined she would be his prey.
My chance gone – he could have been mine.
No time for what I wanted to say,

determined she would be his prey,
she lured him in with piercing eyes.
No time for what I wanted to say.
They both clasped hands, waved goodbyes,

she lured him in with piercing eyes.
I looked his way; he didn't see.
They both clasped hands, waved goodbyes.
But for her, it could have been me.

3. It should have been me

I wished that you would look at me, one time
the way you gazed at her, when we all met.
I really tried to break into your set
but she had you wrapped tight in trails of slime.

Her arms like pincers round your neck she curled,
her flashing teeth, her pointy breasts, her smirk,
her way of dance more shimmy like a twerk,
gyrating round and round your form, she whirled.

I tried so hard to get to you or near,
I moved, then she, like magic, would appear
as though my presence choked the atmosphere.

Her eyes then flashed at me – she drew a line
and wrapped a gossamer-like web, so clearly fine.
She laughed and hissed at me, 'Get back, he's mine!'

4. Me and my Mouse

The sun was hot; I lay down on the ground,
then silence broken by the sound of a mouse,

crawling along me, rooting in pockets,
snuffling and sniffing, looking for some bread.
I cupped my hands round him; called him my pet,
then took him back with me to share my home.

It's only rented but I've made it home.
It's a bit posh really for my background.
You're not really allowed to keep a pet,
some have a budgie, but never a mouse.
These people drink wine and eat fancy bread
served at posh parties, not kept in pockets.

I'm used to coins and tickets in pockets,
always made sure I had my bus-fare home,
for a supper of tea with jam and bread.
That's how we fared on our simple homeground.
'Do as you're told and be quiet as a mouse!'
We had no chairs, no curtains, no carpet,

certainly no toys and never a pet.
Dad brought stolen food, stuffed in his pockets.
Our kitchen had flies and even a mouse
so we never invited our friends home.
You just didn't do that with our background,
Mum down-trodden, Dad sole winner of bread.

Our food was stodgy, potatoes and bread,
I might get an egg, me being Dad's pet.
Nothing was wasted, nor spilt on the ground,
anything over, hidden in pockets.
No creatures wanted to invade our home,

not to encourage some rats or a mouse.

Poor people would eat dead birds or mouse,
we felt lucky to get dripping and bread.
That's long ago; now I've got my own home,
I've got a bathroom, a phone and a pet,
I've got fine clothes with rich silk-lined pockets,
a fancy apartment, built on high ground.

Me and my mouse now both share common ground,
we both love our home and he is my pet,
crumbs of posh bread now stored in my pockets.

THE GIFT

A work of fiction, by Sally Wilson

There was no hint of recognition. Not a flicker in her eyes. She doesn't know me.

'Please. Can you help me?' She is laughing and pointing upwards away from the bridge towards a flickering red banner which clings to the branches reaching out from the embankment along the railway line. 'The wind blew it out of my hands.'

I don't want to speak to her but there is nobody here to help me. I can see the sun sinking into the horizon. Rush hour is over, the tracks empty. It is the lonely part of the evening outside. Inside loved ones are winding down together, drawing the curtains, pulling the blinds down on another day. I reluctantly turn my eyes back to her. Her hair, which had probably started the day in a neat twist, is now whipping tendrils across her face. She struggles to control it as she speaks. She is older than she looks in the photo. A few stray greys, a line or two, shallow still, around her eyes. My gaze follows the woman's outstretched hand. The gold flecks in the cloth suspended in the tree have faded to grey in the dimming dusk light but it is still as beautiful as I remember it from the photograph.

I saw it for the first time this morning in those few precious minutes after Richard had gone to work and the kids had gone to school. My days are mapped out in opportunities. Times when I can allow myself to have a good scratch at that itch which dominates my thoughts. I am always careful afterwards to put his iPad back exactly as he left it.

This morning I entered Richard's log in details and there it was. His life laid out for me to indulge in, satisfying my need to know every tiny detail I think I'm missing. My hands were damp as I tapped the keys. There were the text messages between them, splayed out in front of me, taunting me with their secrets, like a Christmas present under the tree that you want to pick up and feel knowing you may be disappointed with what's inside. The latest conversation had started when Richard was away on business in China last week. Judging by the phrase 'miss you' which punctuated the messages, I knew she hadn't gone with him. It made me feel ridiculously relieved. Silly really. Simply that she didn't always get to have him either. I've read the messages so many times that I've almost memorised them. The insinuated giggles interspersed between lines of innuendos and what seem like tactical arrangements. Confessions of lust pushing an ugly fist down my throat until I have to swallow the bile that tries to force its way up. But despite the nausea I always feel compelled to continue, like picking at a scab over my heart to make it bleed over and over again.

The last entry was new, a photograph and a caption. The photograph was of her, wearing that scarf. The one that flutters there now like a bloodied flag. Bright red diaphanous material with miniature doves embroidered in fine gold thread so that they glittered out at the camera. The caption said 'Your beautiful gift just makes me smile'. I let my breath out. He never brings back presents for me. Not even for the kids. He has always said it isn't a habit he wants to get into. It seems he doesn't always mean what he says. What is it that makes him want to break the rules for that woman? What is so special about her? In all their conversations, he never said he loved her. He reserves that for me.

Richard's work takes him everywhere which is why I hadn't known. The trips away, the work drinks, the meals with clients, they had become commonplace over the years. Plenty of simple opportunities. I could have confronted him. I could have asked him about the photograph my friend had posted on Facebook six months ago. It had shown a group of them with those two standing together, his hand placed just a little bit too comfortably around her waist and her eyes turned away from the camera, fixed on his face. I had known as soon as I saw it. The text messages had just been confirmation. Somehow though it had never been the right time. Rolling the dice to see what the outcome will be. The gamble too dangerous, the stakes too high. I have never been sure the dice would land in my favour.

'What can I do?' The words are out before I realise I am saying them. 'You're a lot taller than me so I don't think I can be much help.'

The woman laughs at that. 'You're lucky being short. You get to wear heels. At my height wearing heels makes me look like Goliath!'

It feels like it should be an insult, being described as short, but somehow it's not. I only wear heels as far as my desk at work, then I kick them off and exchange them for my flats that I keep stowed in my desk drawer. I keep a lot of things hidden in my desk. Biscuits, chocolate, a trashy novel for when I get really bored at work and can't concentrate. Lately I have also been sliding my tablet away when I am mid-search so I can pick up where I left off. It is so frustrating to start again especially when I think I'm on to something. It has become an addiction, the need for information. The poring through pages on the internet. Entering their names, going from page to page, Facebook post to Facebook post in the search for another fix that will take me higher than the last. The trouble is the come down always takes longer. The brooding lingers. Richard comes home to another unexplained bad mood. This woman isn't on Facebook but I see the people Richard is connected to, the faces and names that inhabit his other world where I don't belong. What do they know about him? What are they to him?

I've imagined this meeting, her and I. I've fantasised about what I might say, where we would be, what I could steal from her. Each time it changes. We are somewhere different. The conversation changes. I get braver.

Richard is one of the good guys. People always tell me that. He helps out at school functions, picks me and my friends up from the pub so we can all enjoy a glass of wine, we have a lovely house, two beautiful children and holiday abroad every year. And standing here looking at this woman now, I'm scared I might lose all that. I'm having trouble controlling my breathing. In for four, out for four. The more I focus on it, the more unnatural it feels.

'Can you give me a leg up? I only need a few more inches then I reckon I'll have it.'

'Are you sure it'll be safe?' I'm peering over the railings down at the tracks which are like two silver stripes in the gloom below. It's a long way down and the height makes me feel dizzy. I step back.

'I only need to reach a little higher. It'll be fine.'

'Ok, if you're sure.' I position myself with my back up against the railings nearest the scarf and cup my hands together ready.

'Wait. Let me take my shoes off first otherwise I'll hurt you.' She bends down to unfasten the straps.

'That scarf must be really precious to you, I mean, to bother with this?'

The woman looks up at me. 'It was a present. I haven't had it very long.' She places her warm foot in my hands and steadies herself by holding onto the railing. From my position, I am looking in the other direction. I can't see what she is doing. I had not imagined in all those fantasies that I could be here, with her, doing this and for a moment I hesitate. My hands move.

'Whoa, careful! Just a little bit further. OK. Aha! Got it.'

She lets herself drop back down onto the bridge. 'That's great.

Thank you so much.'

I wait while she does up her shoes. My whole body is trembling. 'From someone special I guess? The scarf.'

She snorts 'I thought so but turned out the bastard was married. No, I just like it.'

I looked at her properly then. 'Did you really not know? You didn't suspect he was married?'

'Why would I? Said he was divorced, no ring, couldn't meet at weekends because he had his kids. None of it seemed that hard to believe.' She fastens the scarf back around her neck. 'Glad to get this back but what I wouldn't give to ring his neck with it though.' She mimes being throttled which makes me laugh. A startling noise in the quiet evening.

'Listen. I know this might seem odd but ... can I buy you a drink to say thanks?'

'Err sorry I have to get back for the kids. Nice to have met you though.'

She looks down at her shoes and fiddles with the scarf around her neck. 'Of course. Sorry.' As she looks up she is flushed.

I turn to go. Richard will be home now. He'll be expecting dinner. I hesitate. I turn back. 'Though... I've got a bottle in the fridge if you're interested?'

As our footsteps chime out together on the metal steps of the bridge I can't help smiling. I am ready to roll the dice now.

MILKSHAKE

A screenplay, by Jenna Young

Cast List

William: mid-sixties, balding-grey hair; regularly dresses as a woman.

Sophie: eleven, nice girl, easily lured wayward by promise of popularity.

Michelle: Sophie's classmate, overly mature, looks and dresses 16; troublesome.

Emma: Sophie's friend and classmate.

Kirsty: classmate, also overly mature, looks older, rowdy.

Marie: Sophie's mum, pretty and stylish; kind.

Phil: Sophie's dad.

Rose: Sophie's elder sister.

Shopkeeper

Waitress

INT. WILLIAM'S FLAT. MORNING.

WILLIAM is in his small and sparse flat that has lingered in the 70s despite it being 1995.

SERIES OF SHOTS/MONTAGE:

A) WILLIAM sits on the bed and pulls natural-tan tights over his legs, red-painted nails clearly visible.
B) He glides his arms into a cream chiffon blouse and fastens the buttons.
C) He sits in front of his dressing-table mirror and meticulously dons a black curly wig. He pouts awkwardly as he draws red

lipstick onto his thin lips.
D) He looks in a full-length mirror and straightens his skirt and green woman's blazer, admiring his appearance melancholically.
E) He exits his flat, with a handbag in the crook of his elbow.

INT. BUS IN MOTION. MORNING.

WILLIAM sits alone on a double seat, near the window. He stares out, despite being able to see very little through the condensation. A teenage BOYFRIEND and GIRLFRIEND sitting a few rows behind and opposite WILLIAM glance over occasionally and giggle to themselves.

EXT. PLAY AREA. DAY.

It's raining. SOPHIE and EMMA, wearing colourful rain jackets, zoom down the street on their bikes. They are happy and laughing. Sophie takes both feet off the peddles and stretches them out in front.

They bump up a curb, one behind the other and meander down a path until they reach a tidy playpark. They jump off their bikes, out of breath, and walk up to the swings.
Sophie kicks one to get the water off. Emma tips one up and shakes it. They decide the swings are too wet to sit on.

                    SOPHIE
          Man.

          (she pushes the swing disappointedly)

          Do you wanna go back to mine?

                    EMMA
          Okay.

They pick their bikes up and walk down the path with them.

> SOPHIE
> I wonder if my Mum'll take us to the
> town-centre.

> EMMA
> When? Now?

> SOPHIE
> Yeah.

> EMMA
> Can't. I've got to go see my Gran later.

> SOPHIE
> Aw boring. I wish we could go by
> ourselves anyway.

INT. SOPHIE'S HOUSE. DAY.

EMMA, SOPHIE and MARIE sit around the kitchen table eating sandwiches and drinking squash. The kitchen is informal and pleasant.

> SOPHIE
> Mum? Do you think me and Emma
> could go on our own to the shopping
> centre one day?

> MARIE
> Emma and I, honey. And no.

> SOPHIE
> But Mummm. Why not? The other
> girls from school do?

> MARIE

STORIES FROM EVERYWHERE – AN ANTHOLOGY

If the other girls pierced their noses
and dangled carrots through as nose-
rings would you do that
too?
          (Emma chuckles)

          SOPHIE
Tut, ughhh. Why do you always have
to be stupid, Mum?

          MARIE
Honey, you're 11 years old. You're not
going to the town centre on your own.
          (she looks at Emma)
And you know your mum'll say the
same.

          SOPHIE
Ochh.
          (she sits back and folds her arms)

INT. SHOPPING CENTRE. DAY

The shopping centre has a steady flow of people. WILLIAM stops at
the Marie-Curie shop window and peers in. He walks on and stops at
a jewellery-shop window, stooping to inspect one or two things
closely. Some passing shoppers take second glances at him.

INT. BUS IN MOTION. DAY

WILLIAM sits at the window again on his return journey. His hand
rests on his grocery bags sitting alongside him on the seat. He stares
through the window.

INT. SOPHIE'S HOUSE. KITCHEN. EVENING.

SOPHIE, MARIE, ROSE and PHIL are eating dinner around the table. There's lots of plates and dishes of food, which get passed around intermittently.

                    SOPHIE
        I just don't understand why we're not
        allowed to go?

                    MARIE
        Uh, Sophie, please. Stop going on
        about it.

                    ROSE
        You're not still talking about the mall,
        are you?

                    PHIL
        The what? The mall? Are we in
        Beverly Hills?

                    ROSE
        Ha ha ha.

                    SOPHIE
        Dad, why can't me and Emma go to
        the shopping-centre ourselves?

                    PHIL
        Why do you want –

                    ROSE
        As if. I was 14 before I was allowed to
        go. And even then, Mum dropped me
        off and picked me up.

                    PHIL
        What's up with the park?

                    SOPHIE

Daaad. All the other girls go.

                    PHIL
What other girls?

                    MARIE
All of them. Apart from poor little
hard-
done-by Sophie.

                    SOPHIE
But I just want to look in the shops …
and at the
ice-skaters and stuff.

                    MARIE
Listen – I'll speak to Emma's mum.
But enough
about it for now, okay?

                    SOPHIE
Yesss.
         (excitedly clenching her fists)

INT. WILLIAM'S HOUSE. EVENING

WILLIAM sits at the head of his dining table, dressed as before but without his wig. He is eating a bland-looking dinner. The house is quiet, other than his cutlery against the plate.

EXT. SCHOOL PLAYGROUND. AFTERNOON.

School has just finished for the day and kids are filtering out
quickly. SOPHIE and EMMA walk towards the gates.

                         SOPHIE
            Has my mum called your mum yet?

                         EMMA
            Don't think so. Mum hasn't said.

MICHELLE walks passed, bumping purposefully into Sophie.

                         MICHELLE
                      (sarcastically)
            Oops. Sorry.

She walks on raucously with KIRSTY and a group of girls following
behind.

                         SOPHIE
                      (looking miserable)
            You comin' for dinner?

                         EMMA
            Yeah, okay.

INT. SOPHIE'S HOUSE. KITCHEN. NIGHT.

MARIE and SOPHIE are loading dishes into the dishwasher.

                         SOPHIE
            Did you ask Emma's mum if we could
            go to the shops?

                         MARIE
            Yes.

STORIES FROM EVERYWHERE – AN ANTHOLOGY

Sophie stares up at Marie in anticipation. Marie puts her hand on her hip, stares at her daughter resignedly and lets out a long sigh.

INT. SOPHIE'S HOUSE. HALLWAY. MORNING.

SOPHIE and MARIE are standing by the open front door.

> MARIE
> Here's twenty pence for your bus
> journey in.
> And one for your bus home, okay? If
> you lose
> it you'll be spending the night there.
> And
> here's £5 – don't spend it all on
> sweets, okay?

> SOPHIE
> Thanks, Mum. I won't, I promise.

> MARIE
> Right then, have fun. And back by 3
> remember.
> > (Sophie runs out)
> Bye.

INT. BUS IN MOTION. MORNING.

EMMA and SOPHIE sit together on the bus, paralleling the position of the giggling teenagers from William's bus journey. They are talking excitedly.

> SOPHIE
> Okay, so should we go to Tammy Girl
> first then?

> EMMA
> Yeah. And then – isn't C&A just

across from there?

SOPHIE
Yeah, I think so. And I want to go to
that shoe shop – you know the one
with all the good trainers.

EMMA
Yeah the one near Woolworths? Oh
I'm gonna
get a pick 'n' mix too.

SOPHIE
And we should see who's on the ice-
rink.

EXT. STREET. MORNING.

The bus drives on; the girls continue talking and planning.

EMMA (O.S)
Yeah. And my mum said I could get
fries and a milkshake.

SOPHIE (O.S)
Good idea. I might get a cheeseburger.
And we should look in Kylie too...

INT. CAFÉ WITHIN SHOPPING CENTRE. MORNING.

WILLIAM (dressed as before but with a floral blouse and pink nails
and lips) is sitting at a table alone. The WAITRESS approaches to
take his order.

WAITRESS
Bacon roll and tea for ya, hen, aye?

(William nods and smiles)

INT. SHOPPING CENTRE. MORNING.

SOPHIE and EMMA are in a girls clothing store, looking at various items. Sophie holds up a white boob-tube.

                    SOPHIE
          What about this? You like it?

                    EMMA
          Nah. You'd never be allowed to wear
          that, anyway.
          Look at these -
              (she holds up a pair of glittered
                    denims)

                    SOPHIE
          Oh yeah, they're like the ones
          Michelle had on
          at the Christmas party.

                    EMMA
          Uh, I love this –
              (she holds up a yellow mini-skirt)

Meanwhile, Sophie is holding a dress up to her shoulders and swishing it back and forth.

INT. SHOPPING CENTRE. MORNING.

WILLIAM meanders amongst other shoppers.

INT. SHOPPING CENTRE. MORNING.

SOPHIE and EMMA are now in a shoe shop, looking around and trying various things on.

SOPHIE
Imagine if we wore these to our end of
year disco – (tottering on a diamanté
high-heeled shoe)

EMMA
Ooo, or these –
(lifting up another heeled shoe)

INT. 'SAFEWAY' SUPERMARKET WITHIN SHOPPING CENTRE. DAY

WILLIAM lifts up a couple of potatoes and inspects them slightly, discarding some and dropping others into a bag.

INT. 'MCDONALDS' WITHIN THE SHOPPING CENTRE. DAY.

SOPHIE and EMMA carry trays, each with a large cup and carton of fries on them, to the long window-bar seat. They slide their trays onto the bar and climb onto the high stools.

EMMA
What flavour milkshake d'you get?

SOPHIE
Strawberry. Is yours banana? Let me
try.
(she sips from Emma's cup)
Hmm. I prefer the strawberry.

While Sophie takes the lid off her drink and swirls the straw around, Emma's attention is drawn to something within the mall. She stares out, her eyes fixedly following something.

                    EMMA
Sophie, look at that woman over
there…

                    SOPHIE
Where?

                    EMMA
There, look. At the Marie-Curie
window.

Sophie gazes in the same direction as Emma. They look increasingly
flummoxed.

                    EMMA
That's a wig.

                    SOPHIE
So it is. Wiggy wiggy.
          (leaning in to look closer)
That's … that's a man.

                    EMMA
A man?

                    SOPHIE
Yeah. You know … like a tranny.
          (knowingly)

Emma looks at her friend, bewildered, then looks back out of the
window.

WILLIAM, carrying a Safeway shopping bag, walks passed the
window of McDonalds, ignoring but not oblivious to the staring
girls.

INT. SOPHIE'S HOUSE. NIGHT

SOPHIE and MARIE are sitting in the living room. Sophie is playing her Gameboy, but appears troubled by something. She stops playing and rests the Gameboy in her lap.

                    SOPHIE
          Mum?

                    MARIE
          Hmm?

                    SOPHIE
          I saw a man dressed as a woman today.

                    MARIE
          Oh?
               (closing her book and looking at
                    Sophie)

                    SOPHIE
          Why? Why was he dressed as a
          woman?

                    MARIE
          I don't know honey. Sometimes people
          do things like that.

                    SOPHIE
          But why?

                    MARIE
          Well … I suppose … why not?

                    SOPHIE
          But he still looked like a man.

                    MARIE
          Maybe he wasn't trying to look like a
          woman.
          Maybe he just wanted to wear

woman's clothes today.

SOPHIE
So, he doesn't always dress like that?

MARIE
I don't know. Possibly. Possibly not.
He might just dress as a woman on the
weekends.
(Sophie looks visibly perplexed)
He's not harming anyone, is he?
(Sophie considers this)

INT. SHOPPING CENTRE. DAY.

The following weekend. SOPHIE and EMMA are leaving 'Kylie',
both peering into Emma's small carrier bag which she is holding
open. They stop outside the doorway.

EMMA
Where should we go now?

SOPHIE
You want to –

EMMA
(gasps)
Look who's over there.

SOPHIE
– go to Woolworths? Who? Oh, yeah.

WILLIAM walks passed, amongst other shoppers. Meanwhile,
MICHELLE and KIRSTY approach Sophie and Emma.

MICHELLE
Wit you two swats doin' here?

(Emma and Sophie are surprised to see
her)

SOPHIE
(haughtily)
Watching that tranny.

MICHELLE
That's your maw.

SOPHIE
It's your dad.
(Emma and Kirsty laugh)

MICHELLE
(affronted)
I did'nie think you babies were
allowed out ourselves, anyways.
Where's your nannies?

EMMA
We got the bus in.

SOPHIE
Same last weekend too.

MICHELLE
Oh did you now? Their mammies've
let them off the leash, Kirsty.
Anyways, we're away to Mackie D's.

KIRSTY
Yous wanna come?

MICHELLE
(she glares at Kirsty then openly
inspects Emma and Sophie)
Come if yous want. I could'nie care
less. Let's follow that weirdo.

They walk off after William. Emma and Sophie follow behind, exchanging an excited glance with each other. As William walks through the mall, the girls can be seen in the background.

> MICHELLE
> Oi, freak-show, your wig's squint.

> KIRSTY
> Is that your maw's skirt?

> MICHELLE
> More like his gran's.

William continues walking without acknowledging the comments.

> MICHELLE (CONT.)
> Oi Mr, you deaf? Your gran wants her
> skirt back.
> (William still ignores them)
> Fuck 'im.
> (they file into McDonalds)

INT. 'MCDONALDS' WITHIN THE SHOPPING CENTRE. DAY.

EMMA, KIRSTY, MICHELLE and SOPHIE sit at a table with their various food containers.

> EMMA
> That he/she freaks me out. It's so
> weird.

> SOPHIE
> Yeah I know, why does he do that? It's
> disgusting.

> MICHELLE
> Och who cares? He pro'aly gets off on

it.

KIRSTY
Aye, I bet he does. The big dirty pedo.
(Emma and Sophie look confused)

MICHELLE
Anyway, wit've you got in this bag?
(she reaches over to grab Sophie's
shopping bag and pulls the contents
out)
A crop-top? Seriously? Ooo, look at
me in my baby bra.
(she holds the bra to her chest)
Kirsty, isn't this the one your five-
year-old cousin got the other day?

KIRSTY
(laughs)
Aye. D'you get it in Mothercare?

SOPHIE
No, it's from Kylie. Gimmie it back.

MICHELLE
Well, it's no as if you need a bra
anyways.
(she flings the top back to Sophie)

SOPHIE
Just 'cause you have to wear a 64
double F.

EMMA
(laughs)
Do you have to buy your bras in
Evans?

MICHELLE

Fuck off. That's where your maw
shops. You're just jealous 'cause
you've no got any boobs. Anyways,
we better go, Kirsty, 'fore anyone sees
us with these two.
        (they stand up to leave)
You coming here next weekend?

EMMA   SOPHIE
        Probably.
            Yeah, think so.

                    MICHELLE
Might see you next weekend then.
                (to Kirsty).
Let's go.
                (to Emma and Sophie)
See yous in school, geeks. Bye.

Emma and Sophie wave as they leave, then turn and smile to each
other, happily.

INT. SOPHIE'S HOUSE. DAY.

MARIE is standing in the hallway watching SOPHIE putting her
jacket on.

                    MARIE
I just don't understand what you girls
find so entertaining about that
shopping centre. Are you not bored of
going there?

                    SOPHIE
        No.

                    MARIE

Well you're only getting £2 this week.
(holding coins out to SOPHIE)

SOPHIE
Awe Muuumm. The bus costs 40p. I
won't have enough for –

MARIE
Hey! You'll get nothing if you whinge
like that. Some kids don't even get £2
a year. You want this or not?
(Sophie nods and takes the money)
And don't be buying any more of that
silly make-up stuff.

SOPHIE
Okay. Bye.
(she runs out as PHIL enters the hall)

PHIL
(shouting after her)
And you've still not cleaned your bike.
What does she find so entertaining in
those dingy shops?

INT. SHOPPING CENTRE. DAY.

SOPHIE, MICHELLE, EMMA and KIRSTY are in Boots pharmacy
using the hairbrushes. Michelle is putting Sophie's hair into a high
ponytail.

MICHELLE
See, dun't she look better?

WILLIAM enters the shop. His face sinks on seeing the girls and he
swiftly turns and leaves.

MICHELLE

There he is. Fuckin' pervert.

                    KIRSTY
               (shouting after him)
Oi Mister. This shop's for women.
You blind? Blind as well as a fuckin'
perv.

INT. SHOPPING CENTRE. DAY.

SOPHIE and MICHELLE walk arm in arm, KIRSTY and EMMA
alongside. Sophie is looking more and more like Michelle. They see
WILLIAM looking in the Marie-Curie window. He flinches on
sighting the girls, but makes an effort to ignore them.

                    MICHELLE
          Freda, your dick's out.

                    SOPHIE
          Burtons is up there, Mister. You know,
          Burtons for men.

INT. SHOPPING CENTRE. DAY.

EMMA, SOPHIE, KIRSTY and MICHELLE pass by as WILLIAM
sips his tea in the café.

                    KIRSTY
          Oi, She-man. When you goin' back to
          the circus?

          The girls fall about laughing.

INT. SHOPPING CENTRE. DAY.

EMMA, SOPHIE, KIRSTY and MICHELLE are loitering near the ice-rink. WILLIAM passes.

> KIRSTY
> Hi Tranny.

He no longer flinches on encountering the girls – he looks determined to block them out.

> KIRSTY (CONT'D)
> Oi, don't be rude. I'm fuckin' talkin' to you.

> MICHELLE
> Wanna hear the song we've writ' for you, Tranny? Come on, girls.

The girls link arms and form a line in front of William.

> MICHELLE/ KIRSTY/ SOPHIE/ EMMA
> Trevor the tranny, doesnie have a fanny.
> Trevor the tranny, dresses like his mammy.
> Trevor the tranny…

He tries lamely to get around the barricade of girls but the line moves as one to prevent him going passed on either side.

> MICHELLE/ KIRSTY/ SOPHIE/ EMMA
> …doesnie have a fanny.
> Trevor the tranny dresses like his mammy.
> Trevor the tranny…

The three girls continue chanting but the sound fades out and the scene slows. Sophie breaks away and watches William struggle to pass. A hint of sympathy appears on her face.

INT. WILLIAM'S HOUSE. NIGHT.

WILLIAM, dressed entirely in men's clothes, sits at the head of his
table, eating dinner. He swallows and lays his knife and fork down.
He starts sobbing into his hands.

INT. 'MARIE-CURIE' SHOP WITHIN SHOPPING CENTRE.
DAY.

SOPHIE sheepishly looks around the shop, lifting up the arms of
tops and jackets, and fingering handbags, while the SHOPKEEPER
watches her reproachfully.

                    SOPHIE
                    (shyly)
        What does that man … I mean woman,
        look at when she comes here?

                    SHOPKEEPER
        You mean William? The poor man
        who you and your feral friends taunt
        every single weekend? That who you
        mean?

                    SOPHIE
                    (head bent down)
        What does she … he like?

                    SHOPKEEPER
        Eh? Why do you care what he likes?
        It's disgusting what you lot do.
        Running around here like wild dogs.
        Doesn't your mum teach you
        anything? Bet
        she doesn't even know where you are,
        does she?

                    SOPHIE

Yes she does.
(she stares at the shopkeeper)
How much is that yellow jacket in the
window?

SHOPKEEPER
£3.

Sophie walks to the counter and empties some coins from her purse.

SOPHIE
I've got £2. I promise I'll bring the rest
soon. Will you keep it for me?

SHOPKEEPER
(she stares hard at Sophie)
Fine.

As Sophie exits the shop, the shopkeeper removes the jacket from
the mannequin.

INT. SHOPPING CENTRE. DAY.

The following weekend EMMA, KIRSTY, SOPHIE and
MICHELLE are standing looking over into the ice-rink. Kirsty is
dropping jelly-beans onto the ice, watching them dissolve. Michelle
is drinking a large cup of milkshake, her sleeve pulled down over
her hand.

MICHELLE
By the way, where were you last
weekend?

SOPHIE
Eh ... I wasn't allowed out.

EMMA
Why not?

SOPHIE
Dunno, just wasn't.

MICHELLE
Weird.

KIRSTY
Has your maw put the leash on again.

SOPHIE
No. What did I miss, anyway? Was
Tranny Trev around?
EMMA
Ehh, talking of Tranny Trev –
(points through the crowds to
WILLIAM)

SOPHIE
Man, he's still got that stupid blazer
on.

KIRSTY
Pure mingin'. He needs to get that
thing in the wash.

MICHELLE
In the fuckin' bin more like. Make
him, Sophie. Make him take all that
women's shit off.
(she holds her milkshake out to Sophie
and indicates towards William)

KIRSTY
Ha ha. Aye, do it.

MICHELLE
Och, I knew you were a fuckin' softy.

Michelle swipes the cup away from a hesitant Sophie and bounds towards William, launching the milkshake at his back. The cup hits him with a loud bang and the contents explode over him. He stops in his tracks and stands still.

Michelle, Kirsty and Emma run off in different directions, laughing. Sophie strides a few paces before coming to a dead stop. She turns back and watches William – her face begins to express a confusion of shame and intense sympathy. Moments pass before he flicks the pink frothy liquid off his arm and walks on.

Sophie turns and runs all the way to the Marie-Curie shop. She bursts through the doors, out of breath and panting.

SOPHIE

I have the pound; I have the pound.
Here, see?
(she slams into the counter and empties
money from her purse)

SHOPKEEPER

Whoa. Slow down. The jacket's still
here. I said I'd keep it for you, didn't
I?
(she lifts the jacket from under the
counter and places it in front of
SOPHIE)

SOPHIE

No. No, it's not for me. It's for the
man … the
woman – it's for William. When he
comes back in. Will you make sure he
gets it?

SHOPKEEPER

Okay.

EXT. SOPHIE'S GARDEN. DAY

SOPHIE is meticulously cleaning her bike, using a toothbrush on the spokes. She looks like an 11-year-old again, without make-up or jewellery. MARIE enters the garden.

> MARIE
> Hey Sophie?
> (Sophie looks up at her mum)
> I'm heading into the shops – do you want to come with me? You've not been for a while.

> SOPHIE
> (she considers a while)
> Okay.

INT. SHOPPING CENTRE. DAY.

SOPHIE approaches the counter in the Marie-Curie shop.

> SOPHIE
> Has he been in? Did he like it?
> (smiling in anticipation)

The SHOPKEEPER bends down and lifts out a yellow bundle from under the counter.

> SHOPKEEPER
> He hasn't been in. No-one's seen him for weeks.

> SOPHIE
> But ... I ...
> (her face screws up in confusion)

Sophie backs away from the counter, bumping into the rails behind her. She walks out slowly, trance-like. She exits the shop and stands in front of its window. She begins to sob – loud, overwhelming sobs. Passing shoppers look at her. MARIE appears and tries to console her, looking around for a possible explanation as to why she is crying.

INT. WILLIAM'S HOUSE. DAY.

There's a single plate, knife and fork in the drying rack in the kitchen.

The dining table is empty, all four chairs tucked in.
WILLIAM sits slouched in bed, covers up to his waist. His arms are dropped by his side – his left hand clutches his black wig. Vast amounts of discarded ibuprofen and paracetamol boxes and empty blister packets litter his bedside table and the nearby floor area. He is clearly dead.

27234519R00096

Printed in Great Britain
by Amazon